BIRDS
OF THE
MIDDLE EAST

Photography by
DAVID COTTRIDGE

This edition published 2006
First published in 2001 by
New Holland Publishers (UK) Ltd
London • Cape Town • Sydney • Auckland

www.newhollandpublishers.com

Garfield House, 86–88 Edgware Road, London W2 2EA, UK
80 McKenzie Street, Cape Town 8001, South Africa
14 Aquatic Drive, Frenchs Forest, NSW 2086, Australia
218 Lake Road, Auckland, New Zealand

ISBN 10: 1 84537 703 6
ISBN 13: 978 184537 703 8

Reproduction by Modern Age Repro House Limited, Hong Kong
Printed and bound in Malaysia by Times Offset (M) Sdn Bhd

10 9 8 7 6 5 4 3 2 1

Front cover photograph: Little Green Bee-eaters (David M. Cottridge)
Title page photograph: Red-rumped Wheatear (David M. Cottridge)

Photographs

Each species in this book is accompanied by at least one colour
photograph. For many species, the plumages of the male and
female are identical, and identification from the photograph
should present no problem. For others, however, males and
females differ, and in such cases we have usually depicted the
male but described the female in the text. Immature birds can
present a problem to the beginner and expert alike. Some
young birds can be quite different from both adult males and
adult females, being generally drabber, with fewer diagnostic
features. Again, where space has permitted, we have tried to
cover these in the text.

Some species also have a different winter plumage from that
worn in summer, the winter dress generally lacking the colour
and finery of that when breeding. Here, we have aimed to use
photographs of the plumage most likely to be seen in the
Middle East.

Contents

Introduction to the United Arab Emirates
by Simon Aspinall

The Middle East offers some of the best birdwatching in the world. This book contains particular information on the United Arab Emirates, situated in the southern Arabian Gulf and formed in 1971 when seven separate emirates, the then Trucial States, joined as a federation. The UAE is a small country of 90,000 sq km, with oil-rich Abu Dhabi the largest emirate by far and housing the capital city of the same name. Tourism forms an increasing part of the country's non-oil sector economy, particularly in well-known Dubai, which attracts an ever-increasing number of visitors. These include many birdwatchers, unsurprising given that many sought-after species can be found more easily here than elsewhere.

The country boasts a bird checklist of some 433 species, of which around 300 occur solely as migrants or winter visitors. Many are rarities, so-called vagrants, and these are routinely found by visiting birdwatchers, while the country's few resident birders, almost exclusively expatriates, are at work five or six days a week. Amongst the 130 or so regularly breeding species are many established exotics or introductions, mostly of Asian origin. The best time to visit the UAE is between October and May inclusive, with migration times often especially rewarding.

The UAE has no endemic species – species that occur there and nowhere else in the world – although Socotra Cormorant is a globally-threatened regional endemic which breeds, while Grey Hypocolius and Crab Plover, sole members of their respective families, are ever-popular targets for visitors. Other species high on any list of species to-try-to-see, other than those already named, are Great Knot, White-cheeked Tern, Chestnut-bellied Sandgrouse, Striated Scops Owl and Hume's Wheatear, amongst others. The UAE is where East truly meets West, where, for example, Crested Honey Buzzard can perch alongside Eurasian Honey Buzzard, Pintail Snipe can share a marsh with Common Snipe, and Indian Pond Heron can be found alongside Squacco Heron.

A wealth of information now exists on the natural history of the UAE, with birds a popular subject. The *Breeding Birds of the United Arab Emirates*, first published in 1996, is about to enter its third edition, this book purposely spelling out the conservation measures required to maintain the country's avian diversity. The UAE entry in *Important Bird Areas in the Middle East* from 1994 is still regularly cited, while *The Emirates – A Natural History* is an acclaimed recent compilation (2005) of everything known about the flora and fauna of the country, and includes full checklists.

Federal environmental legislation, regulation, monitoring and enforcement are all well-established, although each emirate regulates its own affairs regarding site designation and protection. Balancing development and conservation presents something of a challenge, and the former proceeds apace, especially along the coast and offshore.

Several inter-tidal areas are of international importance for long-distance migrant shorebirds and other waterfowl, while many Gulf islands hold vitally important seabird colonies. Twenty Important Bird Areas, IBAs, were documented for the UAE by BirdLife International prior to 1994, but several more have been identified since. A number of protected areas have been established, including two large marine sanctuaries, covering over 5,000 sq km of sea and island archipelago in the emirate of Abu Dhabi. Ras Al Khor, at the head of Khor Dubai, an internationally important wetland, is similarly safeguarded. Many other vital sites remain without formal protection of any kind, but new reserves are certainly in the pipeline, in the mountains of Fujairah, for example.

How to use this book

The birds in this book are presented in what is known as systematic order. This is scientific jargon and it means that, broadly, the sequence progresses from the most ancient species to the most recently evolved ones – according to our current state of knowledge. The English names of birds have always given rise to confusion, for rarely do any two books use the same ones. In this book, we have opted for those names used in *Field Guide to the Birds of the Middle East*, published in 1996 by T & AD Poyser, and *Birds of the Middle East and North Africa*, published in 1988, also by Poyser.

The species descriptions

The descriptions give additional information to that provided by the photograph in order to help with identification.

Common name. In virtually all cases, we have used the same name as that in the *Field Guide to the Birds of the Middle East* or, when the species is not included in that book, *Birds of the Middle East and North Africa*.

Scientific name. Each species has a Latin-based scientific name, recognized throughout the world. There have been some changes in recent years, but again we have followed those in the books mentioned above.

Length. After the scientific name, the approximate length in centimetres, from bill tip to end of tail, is given.

Range and status. Each species account includes a statement on the bird's status in the Middle East (resident, summer

5

Key to corner tabs

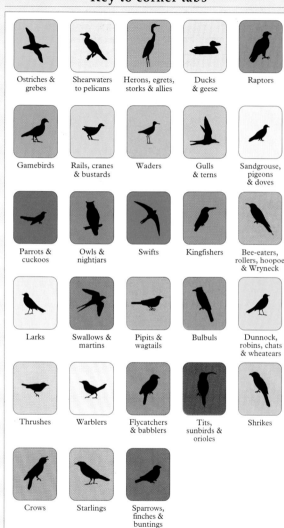

Ostriches & grebes	Shearwaters to pelicans	Herons, egrets, storks & allies	Ducks & geese	Raptors
Gamebirds	Rails, cranes & bustards	Waders	Gulls & terns	Sandgrouse, pigeons & doves
Parrots & cuckoos	Owls & nightjars	Swifts	Kingfishers	Bee-eaters, rollers, hoopoe & Wryneck
Larks	Swallows & martins	Pipits & wagtails	Bulbuls	Dunnock, robins, chats & wheatears
Thrushes	Warblers	Flycatchers & babblers	Tits, sunbirds & orioles	Shrikes
Crows	Starlings	Sparrows, finches & buntings		

visitor, passage migrant, winter visitor or vagrant). In this respect, the Middle East is taken to cover the whole of Arabia and the Levant to the Mediterranean coast, west to Egypt and northwards to include Turkey and Cyprus.

Identifying birds

Identifying birds can often be frustrating for the beginner, and sometimes even for the experienced birdwatcher. This can also be part of the fun of birdwatching: pitting your skills of observation against a creature that refuses to show itself clearly or, when it does, gives you just a back view as it flies away. Most of the birds in this book should be fairly easy to identify, provided a reasonable view is obtained. If you fail in this, however, make a note of what you saw and you will be closer to identifying the species the next time you happen across it.

Your skills as a birdwatcher will improve as you gain experience. To aid this process, you should concentrate on the following aspects.

1. **Size.** It is not easy to gauge size, so it is helpful to try to compare the bird in question with a known species. 'Larger than a sparrow', 'smaller than a crow' or simply 'a very large, tall bird' are all very useful starting points towards a correct identification.

2. **Shape.** Birds of particular families have a distinctive shape. For instance, herons and egrets are rather large, with long neck and legs, and all birds of prey have a hooked bill, while buzzards and eagles also have broad wings. In addition to size, it is especially important to note the shape of the bill and length of the legs. Some features, such as the presence of a crest or long tail-streamers, will often enable an identification to be made immediately.

3. **Colour.** A knowledge of the feather groups is the basis for describing a bird's plumage, and noting the colour pattern accurately is essential for making a correct identification. The stylized drawing of a typical bunting shows these parts of a bird's plumage clearly, and if you want to progress in the skills of bird identification it is essential that you learn them.

No matter how poor an artist you are, make a sketch of any bird you cannot identify and use this stylized drawing to note the colours and markings of the various parts of the bird.

4. **Behaviour.** Watch the way a bird feeds: does it search for insects, or is it a fruit- or seed-eater? Is it a tree-dweller or a ground-dweller? Does it fly fast or slowly? Is it found in flocks? These are all aspects that can assist greatly with identification.

5. **Habitat.** Every species of bird is adapted to live in a particular habitat, and this is an important clue to its identity. Most wader species, for example, are found on the shores of wetlands, including the sea, where they feed on invertebrates living in the mud. Larks inhabit flat, open areas, some species in deserts and others in cultivated fields.

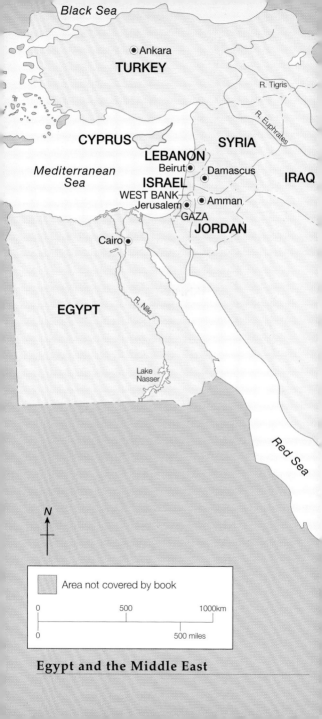

Black Sea

TURKEY
●Ankara

R. Tigris

R. Euphrates

CYPRUS

SYRIA

IRAQ

LEBANON
Beirut●
Damascus●

Mediterranean
Sea

ISRAEL
WEST BANK
Jerusalem●
GAZA

●Amman

JORDAN

Cairo●

EGYPT

R. Nile

Lake
Nasser

Red Sea

N

☐ Area not covered by book

0   500   1000km

0   500 miles

Egypt and the Middle East

Caspian
Sea

ghdad

R. Tigris

Euphrates

Kuwait

Arabian
Gulf

BAHRAIN

Doha

Abu
Dhabi

QATAR

Riyadh

U.A.E.

Muscat

OMAN

SAUDI ARABIA

San'a

REPUBLIC
OF YEMEN

Arabian
Sea

SOCOTRA

Indian
Ocean

6. **Voice.** Some songs and calls are so distinctive that, once heard, they are never forgotten. Most, however, can be quite subtle or can closely resemble those of several other species. While listening to tapes will help, there is no substitute for learning a bird's voice in the field.

Going birdwatching

While it is possible to watch birds without any equipment, binoculars will add greatly to your enjoyment. Later on, you may wish to purchase a telescope. These items of optical equipment can be very expensive, and you should not rush

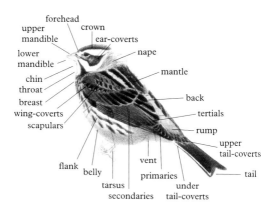

into making a purchase until you are sure of what would best suit your needs. Before you make a decision, it is strongly advisable to test a range of binoculars and telescopes, ideally by noting what your local birdwatchers are using and asking to try them out.

There are, however, a few simple guidelines. Never buy a binocular with a magnification greater than ×10, as it will be difficult to hold steady; ideally, the magnification should be between ×7 and ×10. The size of the object lens should not be less than 30 or the light gathering will be poor. Most birdwatchers use 8 × 30, 8 × 40 or 10 × 40. Always consider the weight, as a heavy pair of binoculars can cause an aching neck and arms.

So far as telescopes are concerned, the best advice is again to see what other birdwatchers are using and ask to look through them. Remember, too, that a sturdy tripod is important, as a flimsy one will move easily in the slightest breeze and this will annoy you intensely.

Where to watch birds in the UAE
by Simon Aspinall

The United Arab Emirates has a wide diversity of habitats: mangroves and mudflats, islands and coral shoals, rocky mountains and wadis (valleys), Acacia and *ghaf* woodlands, and sandy and stony deserts. There are numerous favourite birdwatching sites, some of them man-made, but new sites come and go with some frequency, especially wetlands, which are typically ephemeral. Several reserves are already established, with more being planned. All seven emirates have sites to visit, and the small size of the country means you can reach and return from any site in a single day.

Essential information on key sites can be found on the Emirates Bird Records Committee recorder's website (see details under 'Useful addresses'). Three long-standing Natural History Groups are active, in Abu Dhabi, Dubai and Al Ain respectively, and all advertise their activities widely. The Emirates Natural History Group publishes a refereed journal, *Tribulus*, with articles on migration and other bird research, while the Ornithological Society of the Middle East, OSME, publishes *Sandgrouse* twice yearly; both are recommended reading, with many topical articles.

Coastal wetlands. The UAE has many coastal sites of international importance for migrant and wintering waterfowl. Ras Al Khor, close to Dubai, is protected and has three hides with binoculars and telescopes. Over two hundred species have been recorded here, with Spotted Eagle and Broad-billed Sandpiper regular in winter. Khor Al Beidah (Umm Al Qaiwain) supports many shorebirds, including Crab Plover and Great Knot in winter and on passage. Khor Kalba (Sharjah), on the Gulf of Oman, has the only stand of mangroves on the East Coast, these supporting an endemic race of White-collared Kingfisher, Indian Pond Heron, Clamorous Reed Warbler and Sykes' Warbler. Western Reef Heron is present on all coasts.

Freshwater wetlands. Few permanent freshwater sites exist. Those that do are typically man-made, often arising accidentally, but they may then be managed accordingly. Treated water is used to create these habitats, which are then a magnet for birds. Wasit lagoons (Sharjah) and Al Wathba lake (Abu Dhabi) have impressive bird-lists and each has added several species to the national checklist. Crakes, White-tailed Plover, marsh terns, Bluethroat and Citrine Wagtail are often noted. Visitor facilities are now present at the former site and scheduled for the latter.

Deserts. Nowhere in the desert is strictly off-limits (except oilfields) and birds can be found almost anywhere. You will very likely encounter Hoopoe Lark and Brown-necked Raven, Desert Warbler and Desert Wheatear (in winter), and perhaps a Black-crowned Finchlark or even an Eagle Owl. No matter how experienced a desert driver you may be, try never to go without a second vehicle accompanying you, plenty of water and a mobile phone.

Woodlands. Acacia-clad stony plains characterize much of the eastern part of the country. Again, as with desert areas, access is essentially unrestricted. Just inland of Khor Kalba is a productive area with Yellow-throated Sparrow, Arabian Babbler, Yellow-vented Bulbul, Southern Grey Shrike, Blue-cheeked Bee-eater and Chestnut-bellied Sandgrouse. Similar habitat also lies on the west side of the mountains, abutting sand dunes with *ghaf* (desert oak) trees. Mushrif National Park (Dubai) is a protected *ghaf* woodland, immensely popular at weekends (be warned), but holds nesting Striated Scops Owl and attracts many migrants in spring and autumn. Desert Lesser Whitethroat is easily found in winter. Ghantoot (Abu Dhabi), between Abu Dhabi and Dubai, is an irrigated plantation renowned as **the** place in the UAE to find Grey Hypocolius in winter and spring.

Mountains. The Hajar mountains hold few wadis with permanent running water but are easy to explore, albeit mostly on foot. Take plenty of water. At higher elevations, farms and terracing, mostly now abandoned, can often be found. Lichtenstein's Sandgrouse may be found – best if camped out in Wadi Beah (or Bih), Ras Al Khaimah – along with Chukar, Desert Lark and Hume's Wheatear. Easy of access are the outlying block of Qarn Nazwa (Sharjah), which has nesting Eagle Owl, and Jebel Hafit, close to the inland city of Al Ain, with Red-tailed Wheatear and Blue Rock Thrush (winter), Hume's Wheatear, Sand Partridge, Egyptian Vulture, Barbary Falcon, House Bunting and other typical arid montane residents, as well as plenty of migrants, particularly in spring at the summit hotel. Masafi wadi is another favourite site, with Long-billed Pipit and Plain Leaf Warbler scarce specialities.

Agricultural areas. Irrigated fodder fields are always worth checking. The Dubai pivots and Fujairah National Dairy Farm are just two sites where birdwatchers are welcome to visit, though, as a courtesy, please do ask permission on entering. Lesser Kestrels, Pallid and Montagu's Harriers and a host of tricky larks and pipits will test your identification skills. Indian Roller and Red-wattled Lapwing are abundant, Chestnut-bellied Sandgrouse usually present, and Pale Rock Sparrow regular in spring. Rarities are always likely.

Towns and cities. Many nesting species found in town and city are introductions, amongst them being Laughing Dove, Common Mynah, Rose-ringed Parakeet, White-cheeked Bulbul and Red-vented Bulbul. Native species usually present include Pallid Swift, Little Green Bee-eater, Purple Sunbird, Graceful Warbler and Indian Silverbill. Migrants can be found in almost any green space, no matter how small, with Nightingale, Isabelline Shrike, Ménétries's Warbler and Rufous Bush Robin regular visitors. Vagrants are often recorded too. Safa Park (Dubai) is conveniently located and always worth scouring. Golf courses are productive sites at any time, with Cream-coloured Coursers on the fairways from late summer.

Top sites to watch birds in the UAE

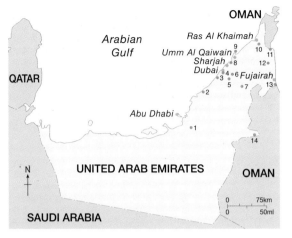

1. Al Wathba lake, Abu Dhabi
2. Ghantoot, Abu Dhabi
3. Safa Park, Dubai
4. Ras Al Khor, Dubai
5. Dubai Pivots
6. Mushrif National Park, Dubai
7. Qarn Nazwa, Sharjah
8. Wasit lagoons, Sharjah
9. Khor Al Beidah, Umm Al Qaiwain
10. Wadi Beah, Ras Al Khaimah
11. Fujairah National Dairy Farm, Fujairah
12. Masafi wadi, Sharjah
13. Khor Kalba, Sharjah
14. Jebel Hafit, Abu Dhabi

Seawatching. Seawatching along the coast of Fujairah has yielded good results in recent years, with Brown and Masked Boobies, Common and Lesser Noddies, Pale-footed and Sooty Shearwaters all having been noted. Persian Shearwater and Sooty Gulls are often numerous, as are White-cheeked and Common Terns, with Pomarine and Arctic Skuas both regular. Red-necked Phalarope winters in large numbers. Certainly sitting in a deck-chair scanning the sea through binoculars or telescope represents a good option during the hotter months! Wilson's Storm Petrel occurs in late summer (July onwards). The Gurfa breakwater, just south of Fujairah city, is a preferred venue.

The near-endemic Socotra Cormorant is best found along the Arabian Gulf coast, including off the Umm Al Qaiwain breakwater, although small groups often sit on navigation buoys anywhere on the open Gulf coast.

13

Ostrich *Struthio camelus* 210cm

The Ostrich, the largest bird in the world, is so well known that it requires little in the way of description. The species became extinct in Arabia in the 1930s as a result of hunting with firearms from motor vehicles, but in Egypt it is still a local breeding resident in the south-east. Evidence based on the remains of eggshell fragments indicates that it was formerly more widespread throughout the deserts of the country.

Little Grebe *Tachybaptus ruficollis* 28cm

A small, rather plump grebe with a shorter neck than the slightly larger Black-necked Grebe. In breeding plumage, note the chestnut neck and the yellowish patch at the base of the bill (the gape). In winter it is a less distinct pale brown, with a fluffed-up rear end. Breeds on well-vegetated lakes, when the bubbling, trilling song is often the first indication of its presence. In Egypt a breeding resident, particularly on the Nile Delta; has a scattered distribution elsewhere in the Middle East and numbers increase in winter, when migrants arrive from the north.

14

Great Crested Grebe *Podiceps cristatus* 50cm

The largest grebe, with characteristic chestnut and black head plumes in summer. These plumes are lost in winter, and it is then dark grey above, with a black crown, and white below – particularly noticeable on the neck. The long pinkish bill, white foreneck and large size separate it from all other grebes. A winter visitor to Egypt, often in large numbers, from its breeding grounds in Europe and Asia, especially favouring saline lakes in the north of the country.

Black-necked Grebe *Podiceps nigricollis* 30cm

A small grebe, in summer plumage characterized by an all-black neck and upperparts with fan-shaped yellow ear-tufts. These are lost in winter, when it is a basically black and white bird with white cheeks, dusky foreneck, small upturned black bill and ruby-red eye. Breeds in small colonies on well-vegetated lakes, but in winter it occurs on lakes and in coastal waters, where congregations of several hundred can frequently be seen. Like all grebes, dives below surface for food. A common winter visitor to Egypt, especially on saline lakes in the north.

15

Mediterranean Shearwater *Puffinus yelkouan* 33cm

Richard Porter

One of the best places to see this seabird is Istanbul in Turkey, where for many months of the year thousands pass up and down the Bosphorus. It is easily recognized by its 'black and white' plumage, long wings, and rapid flight with occasional short glides just a few centimetres above the waves. In good light, it can be seen that the upperparts are brown. In Egypt, small numbers can be seen along the Mediterranean coast, especially in autumn and winter, when the birds wander from their breeding area in the Aegean Sea.

Red-billed Tropicbird *Phaethon aethereus*
50cm (plus 50cm tail)

Richard Porter

An elegant, white seabird with long white tail-streamers, black eye-stripe, black wingtips and all-red bill. Flies rather fast, well above the water, with glides interspersed with quick wingbeats. Usually observed singly or in pairs. Breeds on rocky sea cliffs and marine islands. Resident in the Arabian Gulf, on the coast of southern Arabia and in the Red Sea, where rare on the islands off Egypt.

Brown Booby *Sula leucogaster* 70cm

Richard Porter

A large, Gannet-like seabird with chocolate-brown head and upperparts and white underparts. The powerful creamy-yellow bill, which it uses to catch fish from a plunge-dive, contrasts with the brown head and neck and can be seen at a distance. Juveniles are easily distinguished by the brownish wash to the white underparts. Occurs widely in the Red Sea and is a regular visitor to the Gulf of Suez, at the mouth of which there are small breeding colonies on the offshore islands.

Great Cormorant *Phalacrocorax carbo* 90cm

A large, blackish waterbird which can often be seen in groups, perching upright with wings outstretched as if to dry them. The plumage is an oily black with, in winter, a whitish chin and pale yellowish-green bill. In the breeding season, note the predominantly white head and white thigh patch. Swims low in the water with straight neck, and with bill slightly tilted upwards. A passage migrant and winter visitor to the Middle East, including Egypt, where large numbers can occur on the lakes in the Nile Delta. Within the region breeds only in Turkey.

Alan Williams

17

White Pelican *Pelecanus onocrotalus* 160cm

Although the commonest pelican in the Middle East, this swan-sized waterbird rarely occurs in Arabia, where the Pink-backed Pelican is the breeding bird on the southern Red Sea coast. White plumage, often with an orange tinge, with black flight feathers and a yellow-orange throat sac. Flocks are often seen gliding high in the sky or soaring in warm-air

thermals, especially when on spring or autumn migration. During these periods, large flocks pass through the Nile Valley and Sinai in Egypt, as well as through other east Mediterranean countries.

Pink-backed Pelican *Pelecanus rufescens* 130cm

Richard Porter

Similar to the other two pelicans that occur in the Middle East – White Pelican (illustrated) and Dalmatian Pelican (*Pelecanus crispus*) of Turkey – but smaller and duller, with a darkish crest on the nape. In flight, when breeding, shows a pink wash to the plumage, especially the underwing-coverts, back and rump. This is the pelican of the Red Sea and the foot of Arabia, and it rarely overlaps in range with the other two. In Egypt, it is an uncommon visitor to the coast and the Nile Valley.

Little Bittern *Ixobrychus minutus* 36cm

A tiny, secretive heron, this species keeps to the cover of bushes and reeds and is most active at dawn and dusk. Rarely seen perched, it is most often observed when it flies; note then the distinctive large pale patches on otherwise blackish wings. A summer visitor to Egypt, where it breeds in reeds and other dense vegetation on the lakes in the Nile Delta; Little Bitterns are also common as spring and autumn passage migrants, as they are elsewhere in the Middle East.

Male (top);
female (bottom)

Night Heron *Nycticorax nycticorax* 60cm

A plump heron, which is much smaller than Grey Heron, and in adult plumage is easily distinguished by its grey plumage with black crown and back. In flight the bird's appearance is largely grey. Young birds are brown with streaked underparts and heavy white spotting above. As its name implies, often seen at dusk, when birds on their breeding grounds utter a deep frog-like call in flight. Occurs on well-vegetated wetlands and breeds in colonies, often together with other herons and egrets. Fairly common migrant and winter visitor in Egypt.

19

Striated Heron *Butorides striatus* 43cm

Richard Porter

A small, dark, coastal heron. The adult is identified by its black crown, bluish-grey upperparts and paler greyish neck and underparts. At close range, note its rather marked facial pattern. The brownish immature has streaked underparts and small white tips to some wing feathers, and differs from young Night Heron in its smaller size, dark crown and lack of prominent white spotting on upperparts. The main range in the Middle East is the Arabian Gulf and the Red Sea, where it is a breeding resident. In Egypt, it is found in coastal mangroves and on offshore islands.

Squacco Heron *Ardeola ralloides* 45cm

When perched or when walking, hunched, along the edge of a marsh, the Squacco is a deep yellowish-buff in breeding plumage (with elongated nape plumes) or streaked brownish in autumn and winter. When it flies, however, it is transformed into a basically white bird as the all-white wings predominate. A bird of marshes, lagoons and river edges, especially with reeds and other cover, nesting colonially with other herons. A rare breeder in the Upper Nile in Egypt, as well as in scattered colonies in Turkey and the east Mediterranean. Widespread throughout the Middle East on migration.

Cattle Egret *Bubulcus ibis* 50cm

This small, stocky, white heron is usually seen in flocks in crop fields or grassy meadows, where it frequently associates with cattle. Unlike the other herons and egrets, it is most often found away from water. In the breeding season, the crown, back and breast feathers acquire a strong orange wash and the bill and legs turn red. In all plumages, it differs from Little Egret in its smaller size, its pale bill and its prominent 'jowl-like' chin. Patchily distributed throughout the Middle East but expanding in range, and in Egypt breeds commonly in the Nile Valley and Nile Delta.

Western Reef Heron *Egretta gularis* 60cm

White form   *Dark form*

Slightly bigger and less dainty than the Little Egret, and with two main plumage types: white and dark. The white form is very similar to Little Egret, but has a stouter yellowish (not black) bill and greenish-brown legs (not black with yellow feet as Little Egret). The dark type is easily told by its slate-grey plumage with white chin. Can be very active when foraging, making sudden dashes for prey along the tideline or in rock pools. In the Middle East, it is a resident along the Red Sea (including the Egyptian coast), Arabian Sea and Arabian Gulf, nesting in mangroves and on rocky shores or islands. Unlike the Little Egret, it is rarely found inland.

21

Little Egret *Egretta garzetta* 56cm

An elegant, slim white egret about half the size of a Grey Heron. Larger and longer-necked than Cattle Egret, unlike which it is almost always found by water. It is further distinguished from the latter and from other white herons by its black bill and black legs with yellow feet, which protrude beyond tail in flight. Occurs in freshwater habitats (similar Western Reef Heron lives only on coastal shores and marshes) throughout Egypt and the Middle East in winter and on migration. Small numbers breed in the Nile Valley.

Great White Egret *Egretta alba* 100cm

The largest of the white herons, this striking species with its long neck resembles a large and tall version of the Little Egret, but with a yellow bill and blackish-green legs (no yellow toes). At the onset of the breeding season, the bill darkens and the legs often acquire a reddish or yellowish flush. Occurs in wetland areas, especially fishponds. In the Middle East breeds only in Turkey, but is a passage migrant throughout the region, including northern Egypt where it can occur in large concentrations, often with other herons and egrets.

Grey Heron *Ardea cinerea* 90cm

One of the most widespread members of the heron family in the Middle East. Large and, as its name implies, grey in colour, but with whitish neck and underparts and black plumes behind the eye. In flight looks very big, with broad, bowed wings, and with long neck hunched in to body and legs trailing behind. The slightly smaller Purple Heron has a slimmer, longer, more angular neck and is darker in plumage, being purplish (adults) or deep buff (young birds). In Egypt and the Middle East, occurs on migration and in winter on most coasts and inland waters.

Purple Heron *Ardea purpurea* 85cm

A rather dark heron, similar in size to the Grey Heron, but with noticeably thin, snake-like head and neck. In full breeding plumage it is dark grey, with purple-brown wing-coverts and black streaks on the neck. Juvenile birds are sandy-brown. A bird of swamps, overgrown ditches and reedbeds which is mainly a summer visitor to the Middle East, breeding in scattered colonies in Turkey and the east Mediterranean; widespread on passage, including in Egypt.

Black Stork *Ciconia nigra* 95cm

Similar in size to the White Stork, but easily distinguished by its black upperparts and black neck (with rest of underparts white), whereas White Stork is white with black on the wings. In contrast to herons, which in flight hold the neck hunched into the body, storks fly with neck extended and feet projecting behind. Forms flocks on migration, sometimes circling in warm-air currents, often with birds of prey. The main migration route between its Eurasian breeding grounds and its African wintering area is through the Levant and largely bypasses Egypt, where only small numbers are seen, mostly over Suez and the Upper Nile Valley.

White Stork *Ciconia ciconia* 102cm

Although a pair of White Storks nesting on a roof or similar place is a familiar sight in Turkey, Iran and much of the Levant, sadly, none nests in Egypt. This tall bird, with a large wingspan, white plumage, black flight feathers and reddish legs and bill, is unmistakable. On migration in the Middle East occurs in eastern Mediterranean countries in large flocks, sometimes of many thousands, which soar effortlessly in warm-air thermals. The main migration routes in Egypt are through the Nile Valley and the Gulf of Suez.

24

Glossy Ibis *Plegadis falcinellus* 60cm

Blackish waterbird with a long decurved bill. In breeding plumage dark chestnut-brown, glossed with purple and green; non-breeding plumage is dull blackish-brown, with fine white streaks visible at close range. Feeds in freshwater marshes, by probing in mud and shallow water for worms and crustaceans. Has fairly rapid wingbeats alternating with long glides, and flies with neck extended in front and feet protruding behind, in line or V-formation. A few winter in Egypt, but it occurs mainly on spring and autumn migration, as it does elsewhere in the Middle East, breeding only in northern Israel and Turkey.

Alan Williams

Spoonbill *Platalea leucorodia* 85cm

A white waterbird the size of a Grey Heron, easily told by its long spoon-shaped bill. In breeding plumage has a short crest, a yellow patch at base of neck, and a black bill with yellowish tip. Juvenile has black wingtips and a pinkish bill. Often found in small groups, it feeds in shallow water, sweeping its open bill from side to side to gather insects and small fish. Flies with neck extended, and in 'follow-my-leader' style. In the Middle East breeds in scattered colonies in Turkey and along the Red Sea coast, where, in Egypt, it frequents mangrove swamps and offshore islands; small numbers also occur on migration.

Greater Flamingo *Phoenicopterus ruber* 135cm

Unmistakable, with extremely long neck and legs and curiously shaped bill. Adult has pale pink plumage with black flight feathers, and pink bill with black tip. Juvenile is pale grey. Forages by sweeping bill from side to side through water with head upside-down, often submerged. In the Middle East, breeds in dense, isolated colonies on salt lakes in Turkey, but departs in autumn to spend the winter mainly in coastal areas, especially around Arabia and the salt lakes of northern Egypt.

Greylag Goose *Anser anser* 80cm

Several species of grey geese may occur in the Middle East, but the Greylag is the only one that breeds (in Turkey and Iraq). All are similar, but the Greylag is best told by its large size, large pinkish bill and pink legs. It lacks any distinctive features, whereas the White-fronted Goose (*Anser albifrons*), the only other grey goose to be encountered in Egypt, has a white forehead and black bars on its underparts. The Greylag is an accidental visitor to Egypt, with no recent records, while the White-front is a rare and irregular winter visitor.

26

Egyptian Goose *Alopochen aegyptiacus* 68cm

Tim Loseby

The only goose that breeds in Egypt. Easily told by its greyish-buff plumage with chestnut eye patches. In flight, shows white upperwing- and underwing-coverts contrasting with black flight feathers. This can cause confusion with Ruddy Shelduck, but that species has a wholly orange-brown body and lacks the dark eye patches of Egyptian Goose. Occurs on or around freshwater marshes and usually breeds in hole in bank or tree. Resident in southern Egypt, but occasionally wanders farther north.

Ruddy Shelduck *Tadorna ferruginea* 65cm

A large duck, easily identified by its orange-brown body with paler head and black neck-collar and, in flight, by extensive white on otherwise black wings. The female has paler head and lacks the collar on neck. Legs and bill black. Rather similar to Egyptian Goose, especially in flight, but the wholly orange-brown body of the Ruddy Shelduck prevents confusion. The Middle East breeding grounds lie mostly in Turkey, but in winter many birds migrate south, reaching Egypt as a rare migrant and winter visitor.

Wigeon *Anas penelope* 48cm

One of the most widespread ducks in the Middle East in winter. The male is distinctive with its chestnut head with prominent yellow forehead and crown, and in flight shows white patches on the forewing. The female is less easy to separate from other female ducks, but note the rusty tones, especially on the sides, the dark areas around the eye, and the short grey bill. Wigeons feed by upending in shallow water, but they also frequently graze in flocks on grassy meadows. A winter visitor to many inland waters in Egypt.

Pintail *Anas acuta* 60cm (plus 10cm tail on male)

The male Pintail, with its long tail, long neck, deep brown head, and white breast with white line extending up behind the eye, is a striking and beautiful bird. The drab female lacks the long tail of the male, and is best identified by its long neck, grey bill, and plumage similar to that of a female Mallard (*Anas platyrhynchos*), a characteristic and common duck in Europe. Often occurs in large flocks in shallow wetlands, where it upends to feed. A winter visitor to most parts of the Middle East, including Egypt.

Garganey *Anas querquedula* 38cm

One of the smallest ducks to be found in Egypt. The male in breeding plumage is instantly identified by its chestnut head and neck, with a long, broad, white stripe over the eye and extending down onto side of neck. In flight, it shows a blue-grey forewing. The brown female differs from similar female Teal (*Anas crecca*) in having a whitish patch at base of bill, a dark bar across the cheeks and no white stripe on side of tail. Occurs mostly as a passage migrant on lakes and marshes throughout Egypt and the Middle East; breeds in Europe and Asia.

Shoveler *Anas clypeata* 50cm

The large spatulate bill of the Shoveler readily separates it from all other ducks. Furthermore, the handsome male can be told by its dark green head, white breast, chestnut underparts and, in flight, its blue forewings. The brownish females are similar to other female ducks, but separated by their huge bill and bluish forewing. Occurs on marshes, lakes and sewage-treatment pools. A winter visitor and passage migrant to Egypt and elsewhere in the Middle East.

Marbled Teal *Marmaronetta angustirostris* 41cm

This shy duck is rare and is one of the world's threatened birds. Its plumage is greyish-brown, dappled with pale spots and bars, and with a dark eye patch. Male has a short crest, which it raises in courtship displays. In flight, appears rather long-necked and long-winged. Usually seen in pairs or small groups, often hidden in cover of well-vegetated lakes. It is found mostly on inland waters. In Egypt it is a very rare breeding bird, perhaps with a small number also arriving in winter from breeding grounds farther north, notably in Turkey.

Red-crested Pochard *Netta rufina* 56cm

Male (top); female (bottom)

The strikingly marked male is easily told by its steep-fronted orange-brown head, black breast and undertail-coverts, white body sides and conspicuous red bill. The female is brown, with a dark crown and off-white cheeks. Dives for aquatic plants and small animals, but more frequently up-ends when foraging. Occurs on lakes fringed with reeds and other vegetation, and on marshes and rivers, but seldom on the sea. A partial migrant which, in the Middle East, breeds in Turkey and winters farther south, with stragglers reaching the Nile Delta.

Ferruginous Duck *Aythya nyroca* 41cm

A rather uncommon diving duck, chestnut with white undertail-coverts, the male having a white eye. The female is browner and duller, with dark eyes, and can resemble female Tufted Duck (*Aythya fuligula*), but Ferruginous is smaller, with a peaked crown, sloping forehead and long bill. In flight, shows a conspicuous, wide white wing-stripe that extends to wingtip. Occurs on vegetated lakes, marshes and rivers. On passage, can be found throughout the Middle East, including Egypt, but always in small numbers.

White-headed Duck *Oxyura leucocephala* 46cm

A small, short-necked duck with long stiff tail, which is often held cocked. The male is easy to identify, having a broad, bright blue bill, white head with black crown and chestnut body. The female is duller than the male, with a smaller, greyish bill and a dark bar across the off-white face. Patters rapidly across water surface to take off. This globally threatened species breeds in the Middle East in Turkey on lakes with dense vegetation. Some migrate south in winter, and in the past a few reached Egypt, but there are no recent records.

Honey Buzzard *Pernis apivorus* 57cm

Very similar in shape to Common Buzzard, but has a more slender head and neck, narrower body and longer tail, features especially noticeable in flight. Soars with wings held flat, not raised as on Common Buzzard. Plumage highly variable below, from almost white to chocolate-brown, but most birds are barred; in flight, note characteristic bands on underwing and undertail (two dark bands at base, one broad band at tip). In Egypt, large numbers pass in spring over Suez and Sinai, this being part of the migration route that takes birds over the Levant, especially Eilat, and the Bosphorus in Turkey, as they move between their Eurasian breeding grounds and African wintering areas.

Black-winged Kite *Elanus caeruleus* 35cm

Richard Porter

A small bird of prey, little larger than a Kestrel (*Falco tinnunculus*), but immediately told by its grey upperparts, white underparts, black shoulders and black wingtips. Most often seen perched on trees or telegraph wires, or hovering with rather heavy wingbeats. In open flight, will glide with wings raised in a shallow V. When seen close, its ruby-red eyes are quite startling. Usually on the edge of agricultural areas, but always with trees for nesting. A resident breeder in south-west Arabia and the Nile Valley in Egypt.

Black Kite *Milvus migrans* 58cm

A fairly large, dark bird of prey with long wings and a shallowly forked tail, the fork much less marked than that of European Red Kite (*Milvus milvus*). Plumage dark brown, with paler head and a faint brownish bar on upperwing. Agile in flight, with tail frequently twisted and turned; soars with wings horizontal. Feeds largely on carrion and offal, and gathers in large numbers around rubbish dumps. In Egypt, a local breeder in the Nile Delta and Valley; also a fairly common migrant in spring and autumn, when birds pass between their African wintering grounds and breeding areas in Europe and Asia, on the flyway that takes them over Suez, Eilat in the Gulf of Aqaba and the Bosphorus in Turkey.

Lammergeier *Gypaetus barbatus* 110cm

A huge vulture that occurs singly or in pairs in remote areas. Its long, rather narrow wings and long wedge-shaped tail produce a characteristic silhouette. Adults are blackish above, with dull orange head and underbody; black mask through eye extends into a 'beard' below the bill. Immatures are much duller, with blackish head and greyish underparts. Feeds on carrion, but also takes small mammals. Drops bones from high up to smash them, then feeds on marrow. In Egypt, a very rare resident in the mountains of Sinai and those along the Red Sea. The Middle East population, from Turkey to southern Arabia, appears to be in decline.

33

Egyptian Vulture *Neophron percnopterus* 60cm

A small vulture, and the only one in the Middle East with a black and white plumage. Adult has white body and tail, with black flight feathers, and a characteristic thin yellowish bill and yellow face. Immatures are brown, but have the same broad wings and blunt wedge-shaped tail as the adult; they gain full adult plumage by about five years of age. Often seen accompanying Black Kites at rubbish tips. Breeds throughout much of the Middle East, mostly in mountains, where it nests on rocky ledges. A small population breeds in Egypt, but many pass through the country on migration in spring and autumn.

Griffon Vulture *Gyps fulvus* 100cm

One of the region's largest birds of prey, short-tailed but with long broad wings which bulge at the rear. Distinguished from much rarer Black Vulture (*Aegypius monachus*) by its sandy body and underwing-coverts contrasting with black flight feathers. Soars with wings raised in a shallow V (Black Vulture holds wings flat). Breeds colonially in mountains, but ranges widely over open countryside and deserts in search of carrion. Fairly widespread throughout the Middle East, but apparently no longer breeds in Egypt, although small numbers do occur on migration.

Short-toed Eagle *Circaetus gallicus* 65cm

This large, pale eagle has the alternative name of Snake-eagle, as it specializes in catching snakes. It has a broad head, long broad wings, and a long tail with about four prominent bands. The upperparts are brownish; below, however, it is white, frequently barred brown, with dark wingtips and often a dark head and upper breast. Unlike Osprey and the pale form of Honey Buzzard, which are also whitish below, Short-toed Eagle never shows a dark carpal patch. Soars in warm-air thermals and frequently hovers. A very rare breeder in Egypt, but fairly common on migration in spring and autumn.

Marsh Harrier *Circus aeruginosus* 52cm

Harriers are medium-sized birds of prey with long wings and tail which hunt by quartering slowly over the ground, often making long wavering glides on raised wings. The male Marsh Harrier has a dark reddish-brown body and forewing, the rest of the wings being grey with black tips. The female is dark brown, with yellowish crown, throat and leading edge of wings. A bird of reedbeds and marshes, but on migration it also roams over open countryside. A passage migrant and winter visitor throughout Egypt and the Middle East, where it breeds mostly in Turkey and Iraq.

Pallid Harrier *Circus macrourus* 44cm

Gordon Langsbury; Windrush Photos

Male

Female

The male, pale grey above and white below, with a narrow black wedge on wingtips, is told from similar Montagu's Harrier (*Circus pygargus*) by its much cleaner, paler plumage with black restricted to wingtips. Female and juvenile are brownish with a white band at base of tail above; they have a pale collar behind dark facial border, a feature that helps separate them from similar Montagu's. Buoyant flight, low over ground, gliding with wings held in shallow V. Usually seen over fields and marshes. A migrant through Egypt and the Middle East, mostly in small numbers.

Levant Sparrowhawk *Accipiter brevipes* 35cm

Hadoram Shirihai

A typical sparrowhawk in shape, but with rather pointed wings. The male is easily told by its almost white underparts and black wingtips. The female is less easy to distinguish from female Eurasian Sparrowhawk (*Accipiter nisus*), but note dark wingtips and dark line down centre of throat. This summer migrant to the region is difficult to observe except at 'classic' Middle Eastern migration watchpoints such as the Bosphorus in Turkey and Eilat in the Gulf of Aqaba, where many thousands can pass in a few days in spring and autumn. Unlike the Eurasian species, it occurs in flocks on migration, and this passage can be seen well in Egypt in both spring and autumn.

Common Buzzard *Buteo buteo* 55cm

One of the commonest and most widespread birds of prey in the Middle East at times of migration. A chunky raptor with broad wings and shortish tail, it often occurs in flocks outside the breeding season. Soars on raised wings with tail fully spread. Variable in plumage, but two commonest plumages are dark red-brown or mottled brownish on body and underwing-coverts. Within the region breeds mainly in Turkey, but large migrations occur there and especially in Israel in spring and autumn; it is also a fairly common passage migrant in Egypt.

Long-legged Buzzard *Buteo rufinus* 60cm

Richard Porter

The buzzard of the dry plains, steppes and mountain slopes. Can be difficult to tell from Common Buzzard, but is larger, and has longer wings which produce a more eagle-like silhouette. Variable in colour, but most birds have a dark belly patch, a large dark carpal patch and an unbarred orangey tail; but some can be blackish-brown, with whitish bases to flight feathers and tail. Feeds mainly on rodents and reptiles, and occasionally hovers. Occurs throughout the Middle East, but breeding distribution is patchy and it is rare in Egypt. Although largely resident, a few migrate from the region into Africa for the winter, when it is most likely to be seen in Egypt.

Lesser Spotted Eagle *Aquila pomarina* 60cm

The commonest eagle on migration in the Middle East. Very difficult to separate from the other dark brown eagles occurring in the region, the Greater Spotted and Steppe Eagles, and identification should be attempted only by experienced observers. Lesser Spotted Eagles can best be seen passing overhead on migration at 'hot spots' such as Eilat and along the edge of the Dead Sea, when many thousands may be seen in a single day in April or September/October. These are birds migrating between their breeding woodlands in Europe and Asia and their wintering grounds in Africa; their route takes them over Egypt's Sinai and the Eastern Desert.

Dick Forsman

Greater Spotted Eagle *Aquila clanga* 65cm

One of the world's threatened eagles for which the Middle East has a special responsibility, as many migrate through or winter in the region. A large bird of prey, it has uniformly broad wings which are held flat or slightly drooping when gliding and soaring. Adults are entirely blackish-brown, while juveniles are darker still and have two or three rows of white spots on the upperwing. Differs from Lesser Spotted Eagle in that underwing-coverts are darker than flight feathers. Occurs throughout the Middle East on migration, but always in small numbers. Rare in Egypt on passage and in winter, usually at wetlands.

Steppe Eagle *Aquila nipalensis* 70cm

One of the largest eagles to be seen in the Middle East. Much larger than the Greater Spotted Eagle, and has larger bill, longer wings and more protruding head and neck in flight. Adult is dark brown, with barring on flight feathers and tail. Juvenile easily told from all other birds of prey by broad white band through middle of underwing. Occurs in Egypt and throughout the Middle East (except western Turkey), but only in the winter or on migration from its breeding grounds in Asia, and largest concentrations are best observed in Israel and north-east Turkey; less common in winter.

Imperial Eagle *Aquila heliaca* 78cm

Richard Porter

The Middle East has a special responsibility for Imperial Eagle, one of the world's threatened species, because of the numbers that breed in Turkey or occur in winter. A large, dark brown eagle with long wings and large bill; the crown and hindneck are yellowish, and there are two white 'braces' on the back. Young birds are buff-brown with darker streaks, and have a pale patch on the primaries below. Soars on flat wings, whereas the similar Golden Eagle (*Aquila chrysaetos*) soars with wings raised in a V. Nests in tree. Widespread in winter and on passage in the region, including in Egypt, but in very small numbers.

Bonelli's Eagle *Hieraaetus fasciatus* 60cm

A medium-sized eagle, usually seen in pairs or singly in desolate mountain areas. Adults have white underbody and forewing contrasting with blackish underwing; note white patch on back, though this can be variable in size. Juveniles are buffish below, with usually a narrow dark band through the centre of the wing. Soars and glides with wings held flat, and rather long tail is then a noticeable feature. Very much a resident eagle, tending not to wander far from its breeding area. A rare and local breeder in Egypt, with a scattered distribution elsewhere in the Middle East.

Osprey *Pandion haliaetus* 55cm

David Tipling; Windrush Photos

A fish-eating raptor, seen mostly on lakes or in coastal waters. Dives feet-first for its prey, often after a brief, rather clumsy hover. Easily identified by its dark upperparts and white underparts, with a dark patch at the bend of each wing, and its white head with a dark eyestripe. Occurs, mostly singly, on spring and autumn migration throughout the Middle East; also breeds on beaches and offshore islands on the Red Sea coast of Egypt, as well as the coasts of Arabia.

Lesser Kestrel *Falco naumanni* 65cm

Richard Porter

The population of this small bird of prey is declining seriously, and the species is now listed among the world's threatened birds. Closely resembles Common Kestrel (*Falco tinnunculus*): the female and immatures are virtually indistinguishable from that species, though they are slimmer in build, and have slightly narrower wings and white (not black) claws! The male is more easily told by its blue-grey head (with no black moustaches), blue-grey on upper-wing-coverts and unspotted chestnut back. In the Middle East, a summer visitor to Turkey, Israel and Jordan, where it breeds colonially in buildings, ruins, and holes in cliffs. Widespread on migration, including in Egypt.

Red-footed Falcon *Falco vespertinus* 30cm

Male *Female*

The adult male, slate-grey above and below, is similar to the Sooty Falcon, but note the rusty-red undertail-coverts and red legs of the Red-footed Falcon. The female, with its orange-buff underparts and underwing-coverts and dark mask through the eye, is markedly different. On migration, usually found in flocks. Will often hover when hunting prey; also takes insects in flight by grabbing them with out-thrust talons. In the Middle East, this is a spring and autumn migrant mostly through the east Mediterranean, though generally rather scarce in Egypt.

41

Hobby *Falco subbuteo* 34cm

Richard Porter

A small falcon similar in size to the kestrels, but with more scythe-like wings and shorter tail. Upperparts slate-grey and lacking contrasts, while underparts are heavily streaked dark, with red thighs, and black moustache contrasts with white cheeks. Flight fast and agile, especially when hunting birds; captures insects in flight by snatching them with its talons and transferring to its bill to eat. This falcon occurs widely on migration in the Middle East, but is generally uncommon in Egypt. It breeds throughout Turkey and part of the east Mediterranean.

Sooty Falcon *Falco concolor* 35cm

Richard Porter

This slate-grey falcon arrives on its breeding grounds in late spring and raises its young in autumn, thus enabling it to feed its brood on small birds that are migrating south. It is smaller and more slender than a Peregrine Falcon (*Falco peregrinus*), with long wings and a fairly long tail. The slate-grey plumage is relieved only by a yellow base to the bill and orangey legs. Hunts for prey mainly at dusk. A locally common summer visitor to Egypt (and other southern parts of the Middle East), where it nests in loose colonies in remote coastal areas and desert cliffs.

Lanner Falcon *Falco biarmicus* 48cm

Easily confused with other large falcons that inhabit the desert regions of the Middle East, notably the Saker *Falco cherrug* (which occurs in Egypt only in winter) and the Barbary Falcon, whose breeding distribution is similar to that of the Lanner. This group of falcons is not easy to identify specifically, and even experts can have great difficulty. The Lanner differs from the Barbary mainly in its larger size, longer and less pointed wings, longer tail, and cream-coloured crown (rufous nape on Barbary). Lanner has a widespread breeding distribution in Egypt and the Middle East, but is uncommon.

Barbary Falcon *Falco pelegrinoides* 42cm

Sometimes considered to be just a subspecies of the Peregrine Falcon (*Falco peregrinus*), Barbary is aptly known as the 'Peregrine of the desert regions'. A powerful falcon which stoops at speed on prey, caught mostly in flight. Note the bluish-grey upperparts, buffish underparts narrowly barred on breast and belly, and heavy dark moustaches; unlike Peregrine, it is rusty or buffish across the back of the neck. A bird of semi-deserts and arid mountains, also coastal cliffs. Breeds in the southern part of the Middle East, including Egypt, where it is a scarce resident in the Red Sea mountains, Nile Valley and Sinai.

43

Sand Partridge *Ammoperdix heyi* 24cm

Male (top); female (bottom)

This partridge inhabits rocky deserts, with which its colour blends so well. Noticeably smaller than the Chukar (*Alectoris chukar*), which in Egypt is found only in Sinai, and sandy in coloration, the male with bold, sweeping, black, white and chestnut bars on the flanks; closer views reveal the male's soft blue-grey head with a white patch behind the eye. The female is dull sandy-grey. Often seen in small groups. Can run fast and is most active in early morning, when its far-carrying 'whipping' song indicates its presence. Resident in desolate rocky and stony country, usually near water, in eastern Egypt and many areas of Arabia; despite its name, the Sand Partridge does not occur in sandy deserts.

Quail *Coturnix coturnix* 18cm

One of the region's smallest gamebirds. Rarely seen on the ground, and most often encountered when it is calling on its breeding grounds or is accidentally flushed from grassland during spring or autumn migration. In flight, it looks small, with narrow wings and a striped back; it flies fast, with shallow wingbeats, low over the vegetation. The characteristic song is a regularly repeated 'whipping' whistle, *pit*, *pit-it*, with stress on the first syllable. A common migrant throughout the Middle East, including Egypt, where it is also a scarce breeder in the Nile Valley; small numbers also winter.

44

Spotted Crake *Porzana porzana* 23cm

The small crakes can be hard to separate unless seen well, which is difficult as they are often secretive. Spotted Crake is best told from Little Crake (*Porzana parva*) and Baillon's Crake by a combination of its white-spotted plumage, buff undertail-coverts (quite easy to see when it is walking with tail raised), and yellow bill with red base. A migrant in spring and autumn in Egypt, where it can occur in any wetland areas with reeds and other vegetation; also widespread on passage throughout the Middle East.

Baillon's Crake *Porzana pusilla* 18cm

A small crake, little larger than a sparrow. Very secretive in its wetland habitat, but on migration can sometimes occur in unlikely places such as palm groves, when it is easy to observe and is not shy. It is similar to the Little Crake (*Porzana parva*), which also occurs in the region. Males of both have a bluish-grey head and underparts, and white spots on the back and bars on the flanks, but Baillon's has a wholly green bill (red base on Little Crake) and pinkish legs (green on Little). Occurs on migration in Egypt and throughout the Middle East, but is rarely seen because of its usually secretive habits.

45

Purple Gallinule *Porphyrio porphyrio* 45cm

A large waterbird, as big as a chicken, and easily told by its stout bright red bill, pinkish-red legs and bluish-green plumage. Those occurring in Egypt are of the green-backed form. Feeds on wetland vegetation, which it tugs at with its strong legs and strips with its powerful bill. In the Middle East, there is some suggestion that the shrinking of the marshlands of Iraq (a major breeding area) has caused the birds to spread elsewhere, although in Egypt it has always been a fairly common breeder in the Nile Delta and Valley, where it occurs in swamps with extensive reedbeds.

Coot *Fulica atra* 38cm

An all-black waterbird with a white bill and white forehead shield. Sometimes confused with the Moorhen (*Gallinula chloropus*), but that species is smaller, with a red bill and frontal shield, a white line along the side and white undertail-coverts. Young Coots lack the white shield and have greyish-white underparts. Coots have a scattered breeding distribution in the Middle East, nesting in vegetation at the edge of shallow water. They are also common migrants and winter visitors to the region, including Egypt, where large concentrations can occur on areas of open fresh water.

Common Crane *Grus grus* 115cm

David Tipling;
Windrush Photos

This large, long-necked bird is the tallest species occurring in the Middle East. Its plumage is grey, with a red crown patch, and a black head with white stripe down side of upper neck; a large tuft of blackish plumes droops over the tail. Differs from Demoiselle Crane (*Anthropoides virgo*), which is rare in Egypt, in its larger size and grey (not black) breast. In flight, the extended neck and legs appear to sag below the level of the body. Flies with powerful wingbeats and long glides, and flocks are often in V-formation, especially on migration. Breeds in scattered colonies in Turkey, but occurs throughout the region on migration, including in Egypt, where it also winters.

Houbara Bustard *Chlamydotis undulata* 60cm

The largest traditionally hunted gamebird in Arabia, its numbers have declined markedly in recent decades. Superbly adapted to its desert environment, where its cryptic coloration makes it difficult to detect on the ground. When disturbed, it normally walks away or crouches very low. Long-tailed and long-necked, it has sandy-buff upperparts with dark vermiculations and a black stripe down side of neck. In flight, the black flight feathers contrast with a bright white patch near wingtip. A rare breeding resident in Egypt, largely in the northern coastal deserts and Sinai; formerly more common. Elsewhere in the Middle East, breeds patchily in northern and eastern Arabia; more numerous in winter, when migrants arrive from Central Asia.

Painted Snipe *Rostratula benghalensis* 25cm

This species is unusual in that the female is more brightly coloured than the male. Female has chestnut neck and upper breast, separated from brownish-olive upperparts by a conspicuous band of white from the breast to the back; note also the white eye-ring. In the male, the chestnut is replaced by grey-buff and the upperparts are barred brownish. Inhabits vegetated swamps and reedbeds, but it will venture out into the open. Resident in the Nile Delta, where it is a fairly common breeder.

Black-winged Stilt *Himantopus himantopus* 38cm

A tall-standing, elegant, black and white wader with fine black bill and extremely long, thin, pink legs. It occurs on shallow fresh water or brackish marshes and lagoons, and is very delicate in its movements. Very noisy when nesting or with young. Breeds in scattered colonies throughout the Middle East, but is less common in Arabia; widespread on passage throughout the region, including Egypt.

Avocet *Recurvirostra avosetta* 43cm

A supremely elegant wader, unmistakable with its white and black plumage and long, upcurved bill which it sweeps through shallow water in search of prey. When agitated on its breeding grounds, it utters a persistent, singing *pleet*. Nests colonially, usually in saline areas. Only a casual breeder in Egypt, where seen mostly in winter and on spring and autumn migration; occurs throughout the Middle East, especially on coasts, on passage and in winter.

Stone Curlew *Burhinus oedicnemus* 42cm

A large, brownish wader of dry habitats, this species has a short bill and staring yellow eyes. Very similar Spotted Thick-knee (*Burhinus capensis*), found in southern Arabia, has black-spotted upperparts and lacks black and white bars on the wings. Senegal Thick-knee, which breeds in Egypt (even on roof tops), lacks the white band on wing and has plain rufous or greyish uppertail. The Stone Curlew is a bird of open plains and semi-deserts, breeding fairly commonly in Egypt and other east Mediterranean countries; on migration and in winter, found in small numbers throughout the Middle East.

49

Senegal Thick-knee *Burhinus senegalensis* 37cm

Richard Porter

Closely resembles the Stone Curlew in size and plumage, but lacks the white bar along the blackish band on the wing-coverts. The voice, heard mainly at night, is also quite different, being a long string of loud, piping notes, starting slowly, accelerating, and then descending in tone and speed at the end. In the Middle East found only in Egypt, where it occurs largely along the Nile Valley, nesting on sandbanks and even on the flat roofs of houses.

Egyptian Plover *Pluvianus aegyptius* 22cm

Although this species is now extinct as a breeding bird in Egypt, where it formerly bred in the south, we have included it because of its strong association with Egypt – hence its name. It could still occur as a vagrant on the Nile, as it is found farther south in Sudan. This is an unmistakable and most attractive wader which frequents sandbanks and river margins. Note the delicate grey upperparts, warm buff underparts, and black and white head pattern and necklace.

Cream-coloured Courser *Cursorius cursor* 20cm

A bird well adapted to desert life, and with appropriately camouflaged sandy-buff plumage. Note the head pattern and, in flight, black wingtips above but fully dark underwings. Runs speedily, then abruptly stops and stands upright. Occurs in sandy or stony semideserts, or on cultivation in winter. A locally common breeding resident in Egypt, numbers increasing in winter with migrants from the north. Breeds thinly throughout much of the Middle East, except Turkey; more widespread on migration and in winter.

Collared Pratincole *Glareola pratincola* 25cm

A fork-tailed wader with short bill and legs, in flight resembling a tern. This species has chestnut-orange underwings and a white trailing edge to the wing, whereas the very similar Black-winged Pratincole (*Glareola nordmanni*), rare in Egypt, has black underwings and no white trailing edge; both have a white rump. Inhabits dry plains and baked mudflats, and often seen in flocks chasing flying insects. A summer visitor to scattered colonies in the Nile Delta and throughout much of the western part of the Middle East; otherwise a fairly widespread migrant.

Little Ringed Plover *Charadrius dubius* 15cm

Very similar to the Ringed Plover, both having a complete black breast-band on otherwise white underparts, and a black eye-mask with complete white collar around hindneck. Little Ringed is easily separated by its yellow eye-ring and, in flight, absence of white wing-bar. Mainly a scarce summer migrant through Egypt, where it is also a rare breeder in the north on the margins of freshwater rivers and lagoons. Elsewhere in the Middle East, it occurs widely on migration, with breeding widespread in Turkey but scattered elsewhere.

Ringed Plover *Charadrius hiaticula* 19cm

The Ringed and Little Ringed Plovers are very similar, both having black face markings and a complete black collar around a white neck. Ringed, however, is slightly larger, lacks a yellow eye-ring, and has a prominent white wingbar in flight. It also occurs on marine beaches and shorelines, whereas Little Ringed Plover is more a bird of fresh water. Ringed Plovers do not breed in the Middle East, but are found widely on passage and in winter on all coasts, including in Egypt, where they are often found on inland sites.

Kittlitz's Plover *Charadrius pecuarius* 13cm

A small plover which, in the Middle East, breeds only in Egypt. Most closely resembles the Kentish Plover, but easily told by its long legs, darker, almost brownish, upperparts with rusty feather fringes, and its orange-washed underparts. Often found in small groups and, when disturbed, will first run, rather than fly. If disturbed at the nest, it will bury its eggs. A resident breeder on sandbanks and margins of lakes and rivers in the Nile Delta and Suez area.

Kentish Plover *Charadrius alexandrinus* 16cm

This small sandy and white wader is one of the characteristic birds of the shorelines of the Middle East. It is smaller than the sand plovers, and lacks the complete black breast-band of the Ringed and Little Ringed Plovers; the male is easily told by the position of the neat black markings on its head and its neck side. Occurs on dry mudflats and coastal beaches. A widespread resident or partial migrant throughout the region, but absent in central Arabia. In Egypt, it is a fairly common breeding resident, particularly in the north, and otherwise a common passage migrant and winter visitor.

Greater Sand Plover *Charadrius leschenaultii* 23cm

Larger than Kentish Plover and smaller than Grey Plover, this shorebird is most easily told in summer plumage, when it has a chestnut breast-band and a black mask through the eye. Otherwise rather nondescript, like a large version of female Kentish Plover, but never showing a white neck-ring. Similar to, but slightly larger than, Lesser Sand Plover (*Charadrius mongolus*), which is a rare visitor to Egypt. In the Middle East, Greater Sand Plover is a summer visitor to isolated breeding colonies in Turkey, Jordan and Syria; elsewhere, including Egypt, passage migrant and winter visitor.

Caspian Plover *Charadrius asiaticus* 19cm

This elegant plover somewhat resembles the Greater Sand Plover, but has longer wings and legs, and a smaller head with finer bill. Its non-breeding plumage is similar to that of the sand plovers, but the white stripe above the eye is broader and the breast-band more distinct. In summer plumage the male is a handsome bird, with a deep rufous breast-band bordered black below. In all plumages, the dusky underwing is a further distinction from the sand plovers. A rare passage migrant in Egypt and elsewhere in the Middle East, occurring mostly in fields and grassy areas bordering wetlands.

54

Grey Plover *Pluvialis squatarola* 28cm

Alan Williams

A large coastal wader with a short black bill. In summer plumage, shown by many spring migrants, it is easily told by its grey-spangled upperparts and black underparts, the later becoming white in winter. The European Golden Plover (*Pluvialis apricaria*) and Pacific Golden Plover (*P. fulva*), both much rarer in the Middle East, are always told by their golden-brown upperparts; they also lack the black 'armpit patch' at the base of the underwing that the Grey Plover shows in flight. A passage migrant and winter visitor to the coasts of Egypt and the Middle East; rarely seen inland.

Spur-winged Plover *Hoplopterus spinosus* 26cm

A long-legged, upright plover with black upper head, conspicuous white neck and upper breast, and a black line from bill to black lower breast and flanks. In flight, sandy-brown wing-coverts are separated from black flight feathers by a broad white band: this pattern is similar to that of White-tailed Plover (*Chettusia leucura*), a rare passage migrant in Egypt, but latter has white underparts, yellow legs and an all-white tail. Spur-winged is a common breeding resident in Egypt in the Nile Delta and Valley and Suez Canal region; elsewhere in the Middle East, it breeds locally and occurs on migration.

Sociable Plover *Chettusia gregaria* 28cm

Richard Porter

One of the world's threatened waders that migrates through the Middle East. About the size of a Lapwing, but with a more upright stance, grey-brown upperparts, black crown, long white stripe over eye, and chestnut belly patch which is lost in much plainer winter plumage. In flight, shows a wing pattern very similar to that of Spur-winged Plover. Often occurs in small groups or singly among flocks of Lapwing or European Golden Plover (*Pluvialis apricaria*). A scarce passage migrant and winter visitor from its Asian breeding grounds to Egypt and the region, where it is found in semi-deserts, as well as on cultivated and ploughed fields.

Lapwing *Vanellus vanellus* 30cm

With its greenish upperparts, white underparts and long crest, this is an easily identifiable wader. In flight, note the broad, rounded wings. In the breeding season, its shrill *peer-wit* call is a characteristic sound of wet meadowland. Often found in flocks on farmland, open grassland and lake margins, rarely on the coast. In the Middle East, the Lapwing breeds only in Turkey, but in winter migrants from the north reach many parts of the region, including Egypt, where it can be fairly common, sometimes mixing with other waders, such as Sociable Plovers and coursers.

Little Stint *Calidris minuta* 13cm

Along with Temminck's Stint (*Calidris temminckii*), this is the smallest wader to be found in the Middle East. It has a short black bill and black legs, whereas Temminck's has yellowish legs. In summer plumage, upperparts are spangled chestnut and black, with a pale V-mark on the back; in non-breeding season, it is greyish above and white below. Often seen in flocks of many hundreds, even thousands. Occurs on migration and in winter throughout the Middle East, and in Egypt it is one of the most abundant waders, particularly on coastal mudflats (Temminck's Stint is more frequently found on freshwater marshes).

Curlew Sandpiper *Calidris ferruginea* 19cm

A small shorebird, slightly larger and longer-legged than Dunlin (*Calidris alpina*), with longer, more decurved bill, and easily told from it in all plumages by white rump visible in flight. In summer, a beautiful orange-red from head to belly, with black streaking on crown and back; but in winter pale grey above and white below, thus similar to Dunlin. Usually seen in small flocks on coastal mudflats and estuaries, where it often wades up to its belly in water. Occurs mainly on spring and autumn passage in Egypt and coastal Arabia, where it also winters.

57

Broad-billed Sandpiper *Limicola falcinellus* 17cm

A fairly small shoreline wader, slightly smaller than a Dunlin (*Calidris alpina*), from which it differs in all plumages in having a longer bill with downward droop at tip and shorter, yellowish-grey (not black) legs. Close views reveal a double supercilium. In winter it is a basically grey bird, but in summer rather dark brownish with noticeably dark-spotted breast and sides. Often in small flocks with other waders. A rare passage migrant in Egypt; elsewhere in the Middle East, can be fairly common in eastern and southern Arabia on migration and in winter.

Ruff *Philomachus pugnax* 26cm

Highly variable in breeding plumage, when the larger males have a colourful ruff and ear-tufts of white, black, chestnut or purple. Otherwise a fairly plain wader, greyish-brown above and with buff-mottled white underparts. The head is rather small, the bill dark and the legs usually orange. In flight, which is rather lazy, has a faint wingbar and two prominent white ovals at base of tail. Often in flocks. A bird of inland marshes, rarely seen on the coastal shores. Does not breed in the Middle East, but is found on migration throughout, including Egypt, where it also winters.

Common Snipe *Gallinago gallinago* 26cm

A well-camouflaged wader with a very long bill. The plumage is a mixture of browns, and the face has a dark eye-stripe and a dark bar on the cheek; the flanks are barred. In fast zigzagging flight it utters a rasping call. Much smaller than the rarer Great Snipe (*Gallinago media*) and bigger than the Jack Snipe (*Lymnocryptes minimus*), which is also less common. Rarely seen on the coast, it prefers freshwater marshes and other inland wetlands. Does not breed in Egypt or elsewhere in the Middle East, but is a passage migrant and winter visitor to the whole area.

Bar-tailed Godwit *Limosa lapponica* 38cm

A large shoreline wader with a long, slightly upcurved bill. In breeding plumage (worn by many spring migrants) head and underparts are a deep reddish-brown, this colour being lost in winter, when it becomes streaked brownish-grey. In flight, easily told from similar Black-tailed Godwit (*Limosa limosa*) by its brownish upperwing and white rump, whereas Black-tailed has a broad white wingbar and black tail-band. A bird of coastal mudflats and estuaries. Does not breed in the Middle East, but occurs on passage and in winter, though much rarer in Egypt than around the coasts of Arabia.

59

Whimbrel *Numenius phaeopus* 41cm

A fairly large, brown wader with a long decurved bill. It resembles the Curlew (*Numenius arquata*), but is smaller, darker and shorter-billed, and has a characteristic dark stripe on each side of its crown. In flight, note the dark wings and the white on rump extending up back, as well as, especially, the seven-note trilling call. Often associates with other waders on coastal mudflats and estuaries. Does not breed in the Middle East but occurs on passage throughout, including in Egypt, where uncommon.

Redshank *Tringa totanus* 28cm

A medium-sized wader of the shoreline, identified by its red legs and mostly red bill. In flight, it is noisy and its loud, shrill *tue-ew* call often reveals its presence; it also shows a broad white wingbar and white rump. Nests among tussocks on inland wetlands, but is otherwise a typical wader of coastal estuaries. In the Middle East, breeds only in Turkey, but otherwise a widespread passage migrant and winter visitor throughout, including Egypt.

Marsh Sandpiper *Tringa stagnatilis* 23cm

A medium-sized wader, slimmer than a Redshank, and with slender neck, long greenish legs and needle-like blackish bill. In flight, it shows all-dark upperwings and a square white rump. It most resembles a Greenshank (*Tringa nebularia*), but that species is larger and has a slightly upcurved bill. Rarely found on the coast, preferring freshwater marshes and the edges of pools. Does not breed in the Middle East, but found in small numbers on migration throughout, although scarce in Egypt.

Wood Sandpiper *Tringa glareola* 20cm

Distinguished from the other small to medium-sized sandpipers by its brownish upperparts spangled with whitish spots, its yellowish legs and its straight black bill. In flight, note the dark upperwings and white rump. Similar to the Green Sandpiper (*Tringa ochropus*), but that has much darker upperparts and shows blackish underwings in flight. Often found in flocks, and can be very common. Occurs mostly on the edges of freshwater marshes, rarely on the coast. Widespread on spring and autumn migration throughout the Middle East, including Egypt.

Terek Sandpiper *Xenus cinereus* 23cm

A rather stout wader with a long upcurved bill and short yellowish legs. Very active and restless when feeding, often making fast runs with head held low; constantly bobs tail. Upperparts are pale brownish-grey with black lines on back; plumage is paler in winter. In flight, shows white trailing edge to wing. Occurs on passage throughout the Middle East, but is rare in Egypt; winters mainly on the coast of Arabia, particularly favouring mudflats and mangrove creeks.

Common Sandpiper *Actitis hypoleucos* 20cm

A fairly small sandpiper with short legs and long-looking tail. Its most characteristic features are the white mark between the brownish breast and wings and the almost constant bobbing of its tail. In flight, which is usually low over the water, note the rapidly flicking wingbeats alternating with glides on stiffly held wings. Usually occurs singly or in very small groups. In the Middle East, breeds on mountain rivers in eastern Turkey; otherwise a passage migrant and winter visitor throughout the region, including Egypt.

Red-necked Phalarope *Phalaropus lobatus* 18cm

One of the most easily recognized waders of the region as it swims and bobs on the water, rapidly pecking for food from the surface. In breeding plumage, note the rufous sides of neck and white throat, while in autumn and winter it is white below with a characteristic black patch through the eye. A maritime species outside the breeding season, but occurs also on inland lakes on migration. A scarce migrant in Egypt, but common on passage in the Arabian Gulf and the seas around eastern Arabia, sometimes in very large concentrations.

Sooty Gull *Larus hemprichii* 43cm

Superficially resembles the White-eyed Gull, but is larger and has a stouter, two-tone bill (pale yellowish with a black tip). The head and upperparts are sooty-brown; it lacks the white eye-ring of White-eyed Gull, although it does have a short white crescent above the eye, and sometimes below it. A coastal gull found throughout the year in the Red Sea and Arabian Gulf, especially around fishing ports. In Egypt, it breeds locally on islands in the Red Sea, but also frequents the neighbouring coast.

White-eyed Gull *Larus leucophthalmus* 41cm

Also known as the Red Sea Gull, this bird is endemic to the Middle East. It differs from the similar Sooty Gull in its slightly smaller size and, in adult plumage, its all-black hood and bib, dark grey upperparts, all-dark bill (dark red with black tip, unlike two-tone bill of Sooty Gull) and conspicuous white eye-ring. In flight, shows a dark underwing, like Sooty Gull. The White-eyed Gull is virtually confined to the Red Sea, where it breeds colonially on offshore islands, including those off the coast of Egypt.

Great Black-headed Gull *Larus ichthyaetus* 59cm

One of the largest gulls occurring in the Middle East. Easily told in breeding plumage by its large size, pale grey back and wings, black hood and orange-yellow bill; in winter, the head is white with dark eye patch. Immatures are more difficult to distinguish from other similar-looking immature gulls, but the large size, long sloping forehead, large dark bill and brownish hindneck and sides of neck are helpful. Occurs on coastal flats and occasionally inland lakes. A scarce winter visitor to Egypt, but commoner on the coasts around Arabia.

Mediterranean Gull *Larus melanocephalus* 39cm

Richard Porter

Resembles a small version of the Great Black-headed Gull, but with red bill and all-white wings in adult plumage. In autumn and winter the black hood is lost, and it has instead a broad dark eye-mask. Young birds are difficult to separate from Black-headed Gull, but they are larger, have a black mark flaring behind the eye, and the bill is stouter and slightly drooping. A scarce migrant and winter visitor to Egypt and neighbouring east Mediterranean countries; in the Middle East, breeds only in Turkey, where it nests on inland lakes.

Little Gull *Larus minutus* 26cm

The smallest gull to occur in the Middle East. Noticeably smaller than the Black-headed Gull, and with lighter, more tern-like flight. The adult is easily told by its small size, white upperwings and dark underwings; in summer also by its black head, which in winter is reduced to a grey crown and grey cheek spot. Immatures have a black W-pattern across their wings and back. Little Gulls do not breed in the Middle East, but are winter migrants from the north, largely to the Mediterranean area, including the coast of Egypt, though rather uncommon.

Black-headed Gull *Larus ridibundus* 38cm

Similar to the Mediterranean Gull, but note the slightly smaller size, slimmer, straighter bill, brown (not black) head and black on undersides of wingtips. The brown hood is lost in winter, when there is just a dark spot behind the eye. Often occurs in flocks and congregates with other gulls, especially around fishing ports or where fish catches are brought in from the sea. In the Middle East breeds in Turkey, but otherwise widespread on migration and in winter on all coasts and many lakes of the region, including Egypt.

Slender-billed Gull *Larus genei* 43cm

In winter, this gull closely resembles Black-headed Gull, but is slightly larger. Note that the longer, relatively slimmer bill is pale orange and the iris white, and that the ear-coverts show only a shadow of a dark spot. In summer, the head is entirely white, the underparts have a pink wash and the bill is all dark red. In the Middle East, breeds in Turkey, Iraq and, in Egypt, at wetlands in Sinai; in winter, migrants from the north reach the Mediterranean and most coasts of Arabia, and it can then be quite common in Egypt.

Lesser Black-backed Gull *Larus fuscus* 53cm

A fairly big gull, easily told in adult plumage by its white body and black back and wings, with white spots on wingtip. The legs are yellow and the bill yellow with a red spot. Young birds are dark brownish above, with a white rump and dark tail. A number of different subspecies of Lesser Black-backed Gull occur in the Middle East, and there is much debate as to their taxonomy and status, but all are large gulls with a dark grey to blackish back. Associates with other gulls on beaches and around fishing ports. A winter visitor to all coasts of the Middle East, including those of Egypt.

Yellow-legged Gull *Larus michahellis* 60cm

A familiar gull of the Mediterranean, especially in winter. Fairly large – bigger than the Black-headed Gull – with white body, grey upperparts, yellow legs and a yellow bill with a red spot at tip; the wingtips are black with white spots. Juvenile birds are similar to young Lesser Black-backed Gulls, but not so dark. Like all gulls, this species is gregarious, especially around fishing ports. Breeds on the western Mediterranean coast of Egypt and is joined in winter by the very similar Caspian Gull *Larus cachinnans*.

Gull-billed Tern *Gelochelidon nilotica* 38cm

Richard Porter

This bird somewhat resembles both Sandwich Tern and Common Tern, but its upperparts are entirely whitish-grey, with narrow dark trailing edge to the outer flight feathers. When seen close, the rather stout, gull-like black bill is characteristic. The black cap is lost in winter, when there is just a black patch behind the eye. Unlike other terns, it can often be found hunting insects over the grassy margins of wetlands. A scarce passage migrant through Egypt and the Middle East, with some breeding in the Arabian Gulf and Turkey.

Caspian Tern *Sterna caspia* 53cm

Richard Porter

The largest tern, and easily told by its heavy, bright red bill and, in flight, by the black undersurface of its primary feathers. In winter, the otherwise black cap acquires a whitish forehead and the crown becomes streaked with white. The flight is powerful, and it dives ably for fish from a height of about 10m above the water. The slightly smaller Swift Tern has a long, slightly drooping, yellowish bill and ashy-grey upperparts. Caspian Tern is a locally common breeding resident on Egypt's Red Sea coast and islands and also a passage migrant, mainly in coastal waters; elsewhere in the Middle East, it is commoner on migration.

68

Swift Tern *Sterna bergii* 45cm

Richard Porter

Slightly smaller than Caspian Tern, with narrower wings and more slender bill. Easily told by its darker grey upperparts and yellowish, slightly drooping bill. The Lesser Crested Tern (which breeds in the same areas) is smaller, is paler grey above and has a shorter and slimmer orange-yellow bill. Often in flocks and associates with other terns and gulls. Like all terns, it dives from a height for fish. Largely resident, breeding in scattered colonies, mostly on islands, around the coasts of Arabia, especially the Red Sea and Arabian Gulf, but rare in Egypt.

Lesser Crested Tern *Sterna bengalensis* 40cm

A fairly large tern, very similar in size and structure to Sandwich Tern, but easily told by its orange-yellow bill, while its upperparts are also slightly darker grey and this colour extends onto the rump and tail. Smaller than the Swift Tern, with which it often associates, and with paler upperparts and a smaller bill which is orange-yellow (not greenish-yellow). In the Middle East, Lesser Crested Terns are largely resident in the Arabian Gulf and Red Sea, where they breed on sandy and rocky islands, including those off the coast of Egypt.

Arnoud B. van den Berg; Windrush Photos

Sandwich Tern *Sterna sandvicensis* 41cm

A medium-sized white tern, and the most widespread one in coastal areas of the Middle East from autumn through to spring. Easily told from all other terns by its black bill with yellow tip. In breeding plumage, has a full black cap with rather shaggy feathers on the nape, but by autumn the forehead is white. Note that the rather similar Lesser Crested Tern has an orange-yellow bill. Sandwich Tern rarely breeds in the Middle East (Arabian Gulf), but is found on migration on most coasts, rarely on inland lakes, including those in Egypt, where it is also present in winter.

Common Tern *Sterna hirundo* 36cm

Smaller and slimmer-winged than Sandwich Tern, and with pale grey upperparts. Like all terns, it has a forked tail. When breeding, the cap is black and the bill red with a black tip; in winter plumage, the forehead becomes white and the bill blackish. Usually in flocks, and often hovers before diving for fish. Occurs on inland wetlands in the breeding season, but largely coastal at other times. A fairly common passage migrant through Egypt and the Middle East, where it breeds mainly in Turkey and Israel.

Little Tern *Sterna albifrons* 24cm

This and the rare Saunders's Tern (*Sterna saundersi*) are the smallest terns to be found in the Middle East. Readily told by its tiny size, short forked tail, black cap and eye-stripe with white forehead, and yellow bill with black tip. A further helpful feature is its fast wingbeats. In Mediterranean areas of the Middle East, including Egypt, it is mainly coastal, breeding on sand or shingle beaches, but otherwise found on inland lakes and wide stony rivers, especially in Turkey; occurs widely on passage in the region.

Whiskered Tern *Chlidonias hybridus* 25cm

Can easily be confused with both Black Tern (*Chlidonias niger*) and White-winged Black Tern in winter plumage, but note that Whiskered has broader wings and a heavier bill. In summer plumage quite distinct, with grey underparts which contrast with white stripe on cheeks and white underwings. A spring and autumn passage migrant through Egypt but, unlike the Black and White-winged Black Terns, it also winters in small numbers; elsewhere in the Middle East it is also a passage migrant, with small numbers wintering, being found mainly on inland waters. Breeds in Turkey, Syria and Iraq.

71

White-winged Black Tern *Chlidonias leucopterus* 24cm

In breeding plumage, this is a most striking bird. The black head, body and underwing-coverts contrast with the white tail and, especially, the white upperwing. In autumn and winter it is more soberly plumaged, with white underparts, grey upperparts and a small black crown and ear patch; in this plumage, it is very difficult to distinguish from the Black Tern (*Chlidonias niger*) and the Whiskered Tern. Highly gregarious, it frequents freshwater lakes and slow-flowing rivers. A passage migrant through Egypt and most of the Middle East, with breeding colonies in Turkey and Iraq.

Crowned Sandgrouse *Pterocles coronatus* 28cm

One of five species of sandgrouse that breed in Egypt. Crowned and Spotted Sandgrouse are similar, but Crowned has sandy wings with black flight feathers (Spotted has generally rather pale upperwings) and also has a short tail which is noticeably white-tipped when spread on landing (Spotted has a long pointed tail). The male Crowned has a characteristic black surround to the base of the bill. Both Crowned and Spotted are birds of semi-desert and are resident in Egypt's Eastern Desert and Sinai, where they gather in large flocks at drinking pools; they have a patchy distribution in the Middle East.

Spotted Sandgrouse *Pterocles senegallus* 33cm

Rather similar to Crowned Sandgrouse, but slightly larger, with longer, pointed tail (short on Crowned) and narrow black belly patch. In flight, note also the black-tipped primaries and black secondaries below. Like all sandgrouse, not easy to view on the ground as it is so well camouflaged and remains quite still until flushed. It is best to watch these birds at their traditional desert drinking pools, where they faithfully congregate each morning, sometimes in many hundreds. In the Middle East, the Spotted Sandgrouse has a patchy distribution in Egypt and Arabia.

Adult (top); female (bottom)

Rock Dove *Columba livia* 33cm

The 'pure' wild form of this dove is found typically in flocks in rocky upland areas and on coastal cliffs in Egypt and elsewhere in the Middle East. The highly variable 'feral' form (the typical town pigeon) can be seen almost anywhere associated with human habitation. A medium-sized pigeon, the pure form of which is blue-grey with two black bands on the upperwing, a white or grey rump and a white underwing. It differs from the similar Stock Dove (*Columba oenas*), which is rare in Egypt, in its white underwing and rump and its long black wingbars (short on Stock Dove).

73

Collared Dove *Streptopelia decaocto* 28cm

This pale grey-buff dove is one of the commonest to be seen in several areas of Egypt and the Middle East except in the south of Arabia and extreme south-east Egypt, where it is replaced by the very similar African Collared Dove (*Streptopelia roseogrisea*). Easily told by its pale greyish-buff plumage and white-edged black half-collar. It can often be seen in large flocks, particularly in areas where there is a supply of grain. Frequents towns, villages and settlements and nearby agricultural areas. A locally common resident in the Nile Delta region, and rapidly colonizing new areas of the country.

Turtle Dove *Streptopelia turtur* 27cm

The commonest dove to be seen on migration in Egypt, often in large numbers. Unfortunately, in many areas of the Middle East it is a popular bird for hunting. The most important identification features are the rufous upperparts with black feather centres, the pale purplish-pink neck and breast, and the black and white barred patch on sides of neck. Flight is rapid and agile, and it flutters wings and fans tail during take-off and landing. The song is a soft purring, often for long periods. A summer visitor to the Middle East, in Egypt breeding mainly in the Nile Delta and Valley.

74

Laughing Dove *Streptopelia senegalensis* 26cm

A small and rather dark dove, and the one that is likely to be encountered most often in villages and towns throughout the region. It is smaller and darker than the Turtle Dove, with shorter wings and longer tail. The plumage is a smooth pinkish-brown above, with blue-grey panels in the wing; the dull pinkish underparts have an orange-brown throat speckled with black. Its song is usually of five syllables, *doo, doo, dooh, dooh, do*, with the third and fourth notes longer and higher-pitched. Resident in many parts of Egypt and much of the Middle East.

Namaqua Dove *Oena capensis* 29cm (incl. 9cm tail)

The smallest dove in the Middle East, and in flight reminiscent of a small greyish parakeet. Unmistakable through its small size, long black tail, and chestnut patch in wing when it flies; the flight is very fast and direct. The male has a black face and upper breast and an orange bill. Often in small flocks, and spends much time on the ground. Song is a mournful *hu-hu, hu-hu*. A scarce breeder in the Gebel Elba region of south-east Egypt; elsewhere in the Middle East, is starting to colonize much of Arabia from its stronghold in the south.

75

Ring-necked Parakeet *Psittacula krameri* 42cm

Richard Porter

A bright green parakeet with long tail and heavy, deeply hooked red bill. The male is told by its black throat and the rosy ring around its neck. Often seen in flocks, which are fast-flying and noisy, the birds uttering a shrill, screaming, *kee-ek*. Frequents gardens and plantations, where it feeds on fruits and nests in holes in trees. An introduced species in the Middle East, having originally escaped from captivity. There are now a number of colonies in towns and settlements around Cairo.

Great Spotted Cuckoo *Clamator glandarius* 40cm

David Tipling; Windrush Photos

Like all cuckoos, the Great Spotted Cuckoo lays its eggs in the nests of other birds, in this case in those of crows and Magpies. A long-tailed cuckoo with prominent crest, this species is dark grey above, with wings spotted white, and white below, with a soft yellowish wash on the throat and breast. Young birds lack the crest and have orange flight feathers, noticeable in flight. Favours olive groves and open areas with bushes and trees. A scarce passage migrant and breeding visitor to Egypt and neighbouring countries in the Middle East.

Common Cuckoo *Cuculus canorus* 33cm

The Common Cuckoo lays its eggs in the nests of small songbirds such as buntings and warblers, leaving the latter to raise its young. Long-tailed and narrow-winged, with grey upperparts and breast, rest of underparts being white with narrow grey bars. Females can have reddish-brown upperparts, similar to young birds, though young have pale fringes to the feathers. The call, *cuckoo, cuck-oo*, is a characteristic sound in the breeding areas. Occurs in open country with trees and woodland edges. Widespread on migration throughout the Middle East, including Egypt, breeding in Turkey and neighbouring east Mediterranean countries.

Senegal Coucal *Centropus senegalensis* 38cm

Richard Porter

About the size of a Magpie, with long tail, short wings and heavy bill. Easily told by its chestnut back and wings, black tail, black crown and nape and creamy-white underparts. A secretive bird, keeping to cover, but will sit in the open to sun itself. Flight heavy and low, the wing-beats interspersed with glides. Often located by song, a long series of bubbling notes which descend and then accelerate. Occurs in thick bushes and tall grass, often near water, and in the Middle East is found only in Egypt's Nile Delta and in parts of the Nile Valley.

77

European Scops Owl *Otus scops* 19cm

Alan Williams

A small, slim owl with ear-tufts, and one that is more often heard than seen as it is strictly nocturnal. During daylight, it will often roost close to the trunk of a tree, when its grey-brown plumage, finely vermiculated, and with delicate black streaks on a complex pattern of fine bars below, may be visible. Song is a far-carrying single whistling note, repeated every few seconds, a characteristic sound of summer nights. A summer visitor to its Middle East breeding grounds in Turkey and the east Mediterranean; in Egypt, it is a scarce passage migrant.

Eagle Owl *Bubo bubo* 60cm

Like most owls, rarely seen in the daytime unless discovered at roost or when accidentally flushed. Dawn and dusk are the best times to see this owl, the largest one in the region, and with pronounced ear-tufts and orange eyes. Often the first indication of its presence is its song at night, a far-carrying deep *hoo-hoo*, repeated every few seconds. Occurs in mountains and desert steppes, nesting on a rocky ledge or crevice in rocks. An uncommon resident in the deserts of Egypt, and with a patchy distribution throughout the Middle East.

Barn Owl *Tyto alba* 36cm

This well-known 'white owl' is more typical of open farmland with trees and barns in Europe, but in the Middle East it frequents semi-deserts and oases. The Barn Owl is golden-buff above and white below, with a characteristic heart-shaped face and black eyes. Unlike the other owls that breed in the region, it can be seen hunting in daylight at dawn and dusk, when its rounded wings and slow, wavering flight identify it. A resident of many parts of Egypt, and with a scattered distribution throughout the Middle East. Sadly it is often killed at night by vehicles.

Little Owl *Athene noctua* 22cm

Another small owl, but this one, unlike the European Scops Owl, is often seen in daylight, especially at dawn and dusk. It is rather plump in shape, with a rounded head (no ear-tufts), and frequently bobs up and down, especially when agitated. Plumage is brown above, spotted with white, and white with broad dark brown streaking below. Flight is undulating, unlike that of other owls of the region. It frequents open country with trees, stony wastelands and rocky semi-deserts, nesting in hole in tree, rock or building. Resident throughout Egypt and the Middle East, but absent from sandy deserts.

Hume's Tawny Owl *Strix butleri* 35cm

Paul Doherty

The only owl that is endemic to the Middle East. Being highly nocturnal, it is likely to be discovered by its song, a five-note hoot, *whoo, woo-woo, who-who*. Similar in shape to Tawny Owl (*Strix aluco*), which does not occur in Egypt, but Hume's is smaller and much paler, being sandy-buff with a greyish back, and its eyes are orange-yellow (not dark). A rare resident of rocky deserts and gorges in Sinai, as well as in isolated pockets in Israel and Arabia; recent surveys show that its range is more extensive than previously thought.

European Nightjar *Caprimulgus europaeus* 26cm

Nightjars are nocturnal birds and best located and identified by their songs. Three species occur in Egypt, of which the European Nightjar (which breeds in Europe and Asia) is the one most likely to be encountered during spring and autumn migration. It is the largest and darkest of the nightjars and has a churring song. The smallest, the Nubian Nightjar (*Caprimulgus nubicus*), shows much chestnut in the wing in flight, and has a characteristic song, a double-note *quil-quil* repeated for long periods at night; it breeds in desert areas with scattered vegetation in south-east Egypt, Israel and southern Arabia.

Egyptian Nightjar *Caprimulgus aegyptius* 25cm

Tim Loseby

The palest nightjar to occur in Egypt and the Middle East. On the ground, it is sandy-coloured with paler feather edgings and with fine, black streaks on the crown and upperparts. In flights, appears very pale below, especially on the underwing; above, dark flight feathers contrast with the rest of the pale plumage. Unlike the other nightjars in the region, neither sex shows white wing patches. A local breeding resident in Egypt, and found on migration throughout Arabia, though not commonly seen.

Pallid Swift *Apus pallidus* 16cm

The Pallid Swift and Common Swift (*Apus apus*) are difficult to distinguish. Both are summer migrants to Egypt, but only the Pallid stays to breed, in towns and on cliffs in scattered areas. The Pallid Swift, when seen well, is lighter in colour than the Common Swift, the plumage being brownish with paler flight feathers, and it also has a larger pale throat patch. Like Common Swift, it is often seen in flocks high up, scything through the air for insects. Both species occur throughout the Middle East on passage and breed locally.

Alpine Swift *Apus melba* 21cm

The largest swift to occur in Egypt and the Middle East, and easily identified by its size and its white underparts with brown breast-band. One of its characteristic calls, heard from feeding flocks, is a loud, descending, chattering trill. Like other species of swift, it is thought to sleep in flight. It selects nest sites in rocky mountains, in sea cliffs and in old towns; the nest is a cup of plant material and feathers glued to crevices with saliva. A scarce passage migrant and winter visitor in Egypt; elsewhere in the Middle East, it breeds in Turkey, the east Mediterranean and south-west Arabia.

White-breasted Kingfisher *Halcyon smyrnensis* 26cm

A large, noisy kingfisher, brown and bright turquoise-blue with a white bib, long tail and large red bill. Often seen away from water. In flight, with rather slow wingbeats, it shows a bright, pale blue patch on the wing. Call is a loud yelping, like a whistle being repeatedly blown in bursts. It can be found by lakes and rivers, and also in palm and olive groves, nesting in a hole in a bank. In the Middle East, a resident of coastal Mediterranean countries; in Egypt, it is a winter visitor to the north and probably breeds in the Nile Delta

82

Common Kingfisher *Alcedo atthis* 16cm

A flash of iridescent blue along a river or the edge of a coastal estuary is often the first indication of the presence of this small kingfisher. With a long bill, blue-green upper-parts, orange under-parts, white chin and orange flash behind the eye, the Common Kingfisher is easily identified; it is the smallest of the king-fishers to be found in Egypt. In the Middle East breeds only in Turkey, but birds move south in winter, when it is fairly com-mon in Egypt, occur-ring on the coast and in the Nile Delta and Valley, as well as at desert oases.

Pied Kingfisher *Ceryle rudis* 25cm

A conspicuous, striking kingfisher, unmistakable with its large size and black and white plumage. The male has a double breast-band, while the female has a single one; the crown feathers are elongat-ed to form a short crest. Often seen perching in the open, and will hover and dive into water from a height to catch fish. Frequently occurs in small, loose groups. A resident of the Nile Delta and Val-ley which, in the Middle East, is found also in southern Turkey, Syria and the countries bordering the east Mediterranean.

Little Green Bee-eater *Merops orientalis* 25cm

The smallest bee-eater occurring in the Middle East and, unlike
the other species, it is a resident and most frequently seen in pairs.
Green above and below, with copper-coloured underwing and a
black stripe through the eye. The race found in Egypt has a blue
throat. Occurs in open country with trees and cultivation, nesting
in a tunnel excavated in a bank. Mainly a resident of Egypt, where
it is fairly common in the Nile Delta and Valley, Jordan and southern and eastern Arabia.

Blue-cheeked Bee-eater *Merops superciliosus* 30cm

Slightly bigger than the European Bee-eater, and instantly told by
its turquoise-green plumage with longer central tail feathers. Close
views reveal a dark eye-stripe bordered above and below by blue,
and a chestnut throat. Confusion is possible with the Little Green
Bee-eater, both species having rufous underwings, but Little
Green is much smaller and lacks the chestnut on the throat. A
summer visitor to Egypt, where it breeds mostly in the Nile Delta;
otherwise fairly common on migration, with a widespread passage
throughout the Middle East.

84

European Bee-eater *Merops apiaster* 27cm

Similar in size to the Blue-cheeked Bee-eater, from which it differs in its chestnut crown and mantle, and yellow throat and lower back (the Blue-cheeked is green, with blue, yellow and chestnut on the face). Both species occur in flocks, and their *proop proop* flight calls often indicate their presence overhead on migration. A summer visitor to its Middle East breeding grounds in Turkey, the east Mediterranean and parts of the Arabian Gulf, where it nests colonially in holes in sandy banks; in Egypt, a common passage migrant in spring and autumn.

European Roller *Coracias garrulus* 30cm

Rollers are large, colourful birds with iridescent blue, black and chestnut plumage. Their flight is rather slow, but in the breeding season they have a dramatic twisting and turning display flight, hence the name 'Roller'. Can be noisy, uttering a harsh, grating *krr krar*, especially in flight. Occurs in open woods or farmland with large trees, where it nests in holes. Often seen perched on telegraph wires on migration. In the Middle East, it is a summer visitor to Turkey and east Mediterranean countries; otherwise found on migration throughout the region, including Egypt.

85

Hoopoe *Upupa epops* 28cm

A familiar breeding bird and passage migrant throughout most of the Middle East. With its pinkish-brown plumage, black and white wings and long erect crest it is unmistakable, although it can be difficult to spot when feeding on the ground; it is only when it flies that the full drama of its pattern can be appreciated. Song is a far-carrying *poo - poo - poo*. Nests in a hole in tree or building. Breeds in Egypt, east Mediterranean countries and parts of Arabia; widespread on migration.

Wryneck *Jynx torquilla* 16cm

This strange bird, a relative of the woodpeckers, has a most remarkable camouflaged plumage and a tendency to remain still, making it very difficult to discover. The plumage is generally greyish, with a prominent black band on the crown and back, a black stripe through the eye and a finely barred yellowish throat. Most likely to be observed on the ground and feeding on insects, particularly larvae. A spring and autumn migrant through the Middle East, including Egypt, but never in flocks and nowhere common.

Bar-tailed Desert Lark *Ammomanes cincturus* 13cm

One of at least eight species of lark that breed in Egypt. Most are fairly similar, and good views are needed for correct identification. Bar-tailed Desert Lark is rather plain and unstreaked, and most closely resembles the slightly larger Desert Lark, which can occur in the same semi-desert habitat. Bar-tailed, however, is more a bird of open desert or semi-desert, and differs also in its finer bill and its clear-cut band to the tail. A breeding resident of several regions of Egypt and scattered areas throughout the Middle East.

Desert Lark *Ammomanes deserti* 16cm

A rather featureless lark, similar in size to Skylark. The bill is fairly heavy, with an orange-yellow base. Plumage varies depending on the local rock types, but is usually grey-buff, with slight streaking on the breast, and with an orange-brown tail with a broad, diffuse darker tip; those living in black lava deserts can be very dark. Inhabits arid, stony and rocky slopes and semi-deserts; frequently observed near human habitation. A resident of Egypt, also occurring patchily in Arabia, Israel, Jordan, Syria and Iraq.

Hoopoe Lark *Alaemon alaudipes*   18cm

This lark's tumbling song flight on outstretched black and white wings is one of the characteristic sights of the desert, as also is the accompanying song. On the ground, it is a rather large, upright lark with long curved bill; its plumage looks pale sandy-buff, and at close range black spotting on the breast and black markings on the face may be noticed. When disturbed, it will often run away quickly rather than fly. The song, heard mostly in the early morning, is a series of mournful, flute-like notes accelerating towards the end. A widespread resident of the deserts and semi-deserts of Egypt, Israel, Jordan, Syria, Iraq and Arabia.

Calandra Lark *Melanocorypha calandra* 20cm

Richard Brooks; Windrush Photos

A large lark with stout head and bill and a black patch on side of neck, features it shares with Bimaculated Lark (*Melanocorypha bimaculata*). These two species are best separated in flight: Calandra has all-black wings below, with a white trailing edge, whereas Bimaculated has paler underwings with no white trailing edge and has a white tip to the tail. In the Middle East, Calandra Lark is largely a resident in Turkey and the east Mediterranean, occurring in Egypt in small numbers in winter in open cultivated and arable areas. Bimaculated Lark is a passage migrant in Egypt, particularly in spring.

Short-toed Lark *Calandrella brachydactyla* 14cm

A small lark that gathers in large flocks, particularly on migration. Like all larks, it is a ground-dwelling bird that is often difficult to approach, as the whole flock will rise and move off to a safe distance. To identify a Short-toed Lark with certainty, one must see the pale breast with a dark mark at each side of the neck. When seen well, it is a perky bird, often holding its crown feathers raised, and with a pale flash above the eye. Breeds in steppes, semi-deserts and plains in Turkey, Israel, Syria and Jordan, but widespread on migration and in winter in the Middle East, including Egypt.

Crested Lark *Galerida cristata* 17cm

Probably the commonest and tamest lark in the Middle East, and easily told by its long pointed crest and fluty call. In plumage it most closely resembles a Skylark, but is greyer, with less bold streaking on the back; the bill is also more powerful than that of Skylark. Often seen in pairs at the edge of tracks or dust roads, running swiftly from passing traffic. An abundant resident of Egypt's Nile Delta and Valley and Mediterranean coast, and widespread elsewhere in the Middle East.

Skylark *Alauda arvensis* 18cm

A rather nondescript lark that most closely resembles Crested Lark, but, although it often raises its crown feathers, it lacks the long crest of that species. Generally streaked buff-brown above and paler below, with streaks on the breast. In flight, note the white outer tail feathers, narrow white trailing edge to the wing, and pleasant *chirip* call. In the Middle East, Skylarks breed only in Turkey, but in winter migrants from the north move into many parts of the region, including Egypt.

Temminck's Horned Lark *Eremophila bilopha* 14cm

Probably the most colourful lark of the desert. Identified by its sandy upperparts and white underparts, with striking black and white face and breast patterns. Rather similar to the Shore Lark (*Eremophila alpestris*), which does not occur in Egypt but is found in the mountains of northern Israel and Turkey; it is greyish above, with the face yellow and black (not white and black). Both have short 'horns' at the rear of the crown, and are fairly tame and easily approached. Temminck's Horned Lark is largely resident in the stony and sandy deserts of northern Egypt, southern Israel and northern Arabia.

Sand Martin *Riparia riparia* 12cm

Alen Williams

This small martin is often found in flocks, both when breeding and on migration. The upperparts are brown, and the underparts white with a brown band across the breast. On migration, it will often congregate with other martins and swallows. At its breeding sites it excavates a nesting burrow in sandy or earth banks. A passage migrant through Egypt to its Middle East breeding grounds in Turkey and north Syria; there is also a large migrant breeding population in Egypt along the Nile and in the Delta.

African Rock Martin *Ptyonoprogne obsoleta* 13cm

Rather like a chunky Sand Martin in structure, but entirely buffish on the underbody and lacking a breast-band. In plumage it resembles the Crag Martin, but is smaller, paler and greyer above, and with paler underwing-coverts; the underparts are buffish-white, shading to pale grey, and the chin lacks the dark spotting of the Crag Martin. Both have noticeable white spots on the spread tail. The African Rock Martin is a common breeding resident of desert areas with gorges and ravines in eastern Egypt; elsewhere in the Middle East, it occurs from southern Israel southwards.

91

Crag Martin *Ptyonoprogne rupestris* 14cm

The Crag Martin is very similar to the African Rock Martin, and distinguishing the two can be difficult. In Egypt, most birds are likely to be African Rock Martins, as the Crag Martin is a rather uncommon winter visitor. It is slightly larger than the African Rock, with darker, browner plumage, duskier underparts and darker underwing-coverts. In the Middle East, the Crag Martin is more northerly in its distribution, breeding mostly in the mountains of Turkey, northern Israel and adjacent Lebanon and Syria; there is some southward migration in winter.

Barn Swallow *Hirundo rustica* 20cm

With its blue upperparts and long tail-streamers, can be confused only with Red-rumped Swallow, but easily told by its uniform upperparts (no pale rump) and red and blue on throat. In addition to the migratory races that pass in large numbers through Egypt and the Middle East to and from their Eurasian breeding grounds, there is a distinctive resident race in Egypt known as Mosque Swallow, which has deep brick-red underparts and underwing-coverts. During migration, swallows and martins often congregate in large flocks to feed on insects, particularly over wetlands, where they roost communally in reedbeds and lakeside trees.

Red-rumped Swallow *Hirundo daurica* 17cm

Superficially resembles Barn Swallow, but told by its pale orange rump and nape, the latter separating blue back from blue cap; the underparts are buffish-white. Also more leisurely in flight, with longer periods of gliding. Less prone to flocking than other swallows and martins, and frequently seen in pairs. The nest, cup-shaped with an entrance tunnel, is made of mud and sited under a bridge or in a building or cave. In the Middle East, a summer visitor to Turkey and parts of the east Mediterranean, but resident in south-west Arabia; found on migration throughout the region, including Egypt.

Tawny Pipit *Anthus campestris* 16.5cm

A fairly large, rather upright pipit, similar in size to a Yellow Wagtail. Sandy-buff plumage, that of adult being virtually unstreaked; young birds are lightly spotted or streaked on breast. It can be confused with Long-billed Pipit (*Anthus similis*), which does not occur in Egypt, and also with Richard's Pipit (*Anthus richardi*), which is a scarce migrant and winter visitor to Egypt. Richard's, however, is larger, with longer legs and heavier bill, and has dark streaks on the breast and the mantle. The Tawny Pipit is a summer visitor to its Middle East breeding grounds in Turkey and the east Mediterranean, passing through Egypt and other parts of the region on migration.

93

Meadow Pipit *Anthus pratensis* 15cm

One of the smallest pipits to occur in the Middle East, but only as a winter visitor. It closely resembles the Red-throated Pipit in winter plumage, and also the Tree Pipit (*Anthus trivialis*), which breeds in Turkey and migrates through the region. The best way to tell them apart is by their flight calls: the Meadow utters a short *pseet*, usually two or three times, whereas Tree Pipit's call is a rather high-pitched, buzzing *pzzzt*. Both are olive-brown above and buffish below, with dark streaking. The Meadow Pipit is fairly common in Egypt in winter.

Red-throated Pipit *Anthus cervinus* 15cm

A small, streaked brownish bird that frequents open grassland and the edges of pools and marshes, always on the ground. In summer plumage, easily told by its brick-red throat and upper breast. Otherwise heavily streaked brown, black and buff and thus very similar to the Meadow Pipit (which see) and Tree Pipit (*Anthus trivialis*), which also occur in Egypt on migration. Often found in small flocks and, when flushed, has a very high, thin *speeee* flight call. The Red-throated Pipit does not breed in the Middle East, but occurs widely on migration, including in Egypt.

Water Pipit *Anthus spinoletta* 17cm

Slightly larger than the Meadow and Red-throated Pipits, with which it frequently associates in winter. In summer plumage, shows salmon-pink underparts, greyish upperparts, a white flash above the eye and two narrow white wingbars; in winter, the plumage is drabber and the breast more streaked. In the Middle East, Water Pipits breed only in the mountains of Turkey but migrate south in winter, when they reach the east Mediterranean and northern Egypt, where they can be found at the edges of lakes and other wetlands.

Yellow Wagtail *Motacilla flava* 16.5cm

The Yellow Wagtail complex comprises a number of different races. One of these is a common breeding resident, especially in the Nile Delta and Valley, and four are recorded commonly on migration. The males can be differentiated by their head colour, that of the race breeding in Egypt being greenish-grey with blackish ear-coverts. One of the commonest migrants, the so-called Black-headed Wagtail (illustrated), has a glossy black head and is the only race to breed in the Middle East outside Egypt; the other races, all of which occur throughout the region on migration, have head colour varying from all yellow to all dark grey, with or without a white stripe over the eye. These wagtails can be found on flat areas, especially grasslands near water.

Male (top); female (bottom)

Grey Wagtail *Motacilla cinerea* 18cm

Superficially resembles a Yellow Wagtail, but has a longer tail, entirely grey back and dark wings, and the male in summer has a black throat. Unlike Yellow Wagtails, it is never seen in flocks. Has rather exaggerated movements of its body and tail when feeding, usually on the edge of a river. Utters a high-pitched, metallic call, which often first attracts one to it. In the Middle East breeds only on streams in hills in Turkey and northern Iraq, but is widespread on migration and in winter throughout the region, including Egypt.

White Wagtail *Motacilla alba* 17.5cm

Its pied plumage with grey back and long, frequently wagged tail easily identify this active, ground-dwelling species. In slightly undulating flight, frequently utters a melodious *cher-it* call. Juveniles are much plainer grey, and their head markings are just a shadow of those shown by the adult. White Wagtails are found in most open habitats, but especially on flat areas near water. In the Middle East, breeds in Turkey and parts of the east Mediterranean, nesting in ruins, bridges and crevices in buildings; widespread and common throughout the region, including Egypt, on migration and in winter, when often roosts in large, dense flocks on trees or buildings.

African Pied Wagtail *Motacilla aguimp* 20cm

David Tipling; Windrush Photos

This large, handsome wagtail's most noticeable plumage features are the long white stripe above the eye, the broad black necklace and the large white patch in the wing. It occurs on the edges of lakes and similar wetlands, nesting in a hole or suitable crevice in a building or similar structure. In the Middle East it is found only in Egypt, where it occurs as a rare resident in the Lake Nasser region in the south of the country.

Yellow-vented Bulbul *Pycnonotus xanthopygos* 19cm

One of the typical birds of well-vegetated areas of Egypt's Sinai, as well as the eastern Mediterranean, southern Turkey and Arabia. Like a small thrush with fairly long tail and 'floppy' actions. The sooty head and throat merge into the grey upperparts and pale grey underparts; the tail is blackish. Note especially the white eye-ring and yellow undertail-coverts. Fairly tame and noisy, its characteristic song and call notes have a flute-like quality that is easily remembered: *bli-bli-bli-bli*. A resident, frequenting trees, bushes, scrub, palm groves and town centres, usually in pairs.

Common Bulbul *Pycnonotus barbatus* 19cm

René Pop

Similar in size to Yellow-vented Bulbul, which it also resembles in its actions. A rather drab bulbul with its grey-brown upperparts, sooty head and dirty buff underparts. It lacks the eye-ring of Yellow-vented, as well as the latter's yellow undertail-coverts. Like all bulbuls, it occurs in places with trees and shrubs, as well as in oases and scrub in semi-deserts. Breeds in the Middle East only in Egypt's Nile Delta and Valley, where it is resident.

Dunnock *Prunella modularis* 14cm

An unobtrusive grey-brown bird that spends most of its time on the ground, where it moves with shuffling and rather jerky actions. It superficially resembles a sparrow, but the rufous-brown upper parts are dark-streaked and the head and underparts largely greyish. The bill is fine, not chunky like a sparrow's. Migrant Dunnocks from their breeding grounds in Europe and Asia reach Egypt and neighbouring parts of the Middle East in winter, but they are never common. Breeds in northern Turkey.

Rufous Bush Robin *Cercotrichas galactotes* 15.5cm

A small bird, the size of a small thrush, the Rufous Bush Robin's most noticeable feature is its rufous tail with broad white tips to the feathers. These white tips, especially obvious below, can be observed most readily when the tail is raised and spread, which it frequently is. Otherwise, a pale grey-brown bird with pale stripe above the eye and pale fringes to the wing feathers. Occurs in rather open, dry country with scrub, olive groves and prickly pear. A breeding summer visitor to Egypt and neighbouring countries of the Middle East, and found throughout the region on migration.

Robin *Erithacus rubecula* 14cm

Very few birds can be confused with the plump Robin with its red breast and brown upperparts. Observed mostly on the ground in the shade of trees and shrubs, where it searches for insects, worms and other invertebrates; note then the rather upright stance and bold hopping movements. In the Middle East Robins breed only in northern Turkey, but in winter migrants invade the region from the north, when they occur throughout the Mediterranean region, including Egypt.

Thrush Nightingale *Luscinia luscinia* 16cm

The Thrush Nightingale and Common Nightingale (*Luscinia megarhynchos*) are almost alike. They both resemble a small thrush with brownish upperparts and rusty-coloured tail. Thrush Nightingale, the duller of the two species, has distinct mottling on its greyish breast, whereas the Common Nightingale has clean greyish-white underparts. Both are very skulking and difficult to see. The Common Nightingale breeds in the Middle East from Israel northwards, where it is best located by its striking, rich, musical song; it is a passage migrant through Egypt. Thrush Nightingale occurs only on migration.

Bluethroat *Luscinia svecica* 14cm

Male Bluethroats are very easily told in breeding plumage by their blue bib with an orange or white spot in the centre. Females and males in winter are less obvious, but look for the reddish colour at the sides of the tail base, the white stripe above the eye and the blackish necklace. Mainly a ground-dwelling bird, most often seen near water and swampy areas with thick vegetation and reeds. A common passage migrant and winter visitor to Egypt and other areas of the Middle East. Breeds in eastern Turkey.

Common Redstart *Phoenicurus phoenicurus* 14cm

The male Common Redstart in breeding plumage is a handsome bird, and easily recognized by its black face, white forehead, and rusty-red underparts and tail, the latter frequently quivered. The race that breeds in the Middle East also shows a white wing panel. Females can be confused with female Black Redstarts, but never show the drab grey colour of that species. In the region breeds only in Turkey, to which it is a summer visitor; elsewhere, including Egypt, it is widespread on migration.

Black Redstart *Phoenicurus ochruros* 15cm

Male   *Juvenile*

The male is identified by smoky-grey upperparts, black breast, deep red lower breast and belly, and reddish tail which is frequently quivered; the extent of red on underparts can vary. The similar Common Redstart has a white forehead, black confined to chin and throat, and pale grey upperparts. Both species can show a white flash in the wing. Females of the two are less easy to separate, but female Black Redstarts are more dusky grey. In the Middle East, largely a summer visitor to its breeding grounds in the mountains of Turkey, Syria and Israel; common on migration and in winter throughout much of the region, including Egypt.

Blackstart *Cercomela melanura* 15cm

A rather featureless grey chat with an all-black tail, the latter frequently spread outwards at the same time as the bird half-spreads its wings. Usually seen in pairs in rocky wadis or desert edges with scattered bushes. Has a melancholy song of short, deep, flute-like phrases and whistles, and often allows a close approach. A locally common breeding bird of Egypt's Sinai and Gebel Elba region; elsewhere in the Middle East, it is a resident of Israel, Jordan and the Red Sea coastlands.

Whinchat *Saxicola rubetra* 13cm

Adult

Juvenile

A short-tailed chat most closely resembling Stonechat, from which it differs mainly in its prominent pale supercilium (white on summer male), white patches at base of tail and streaked rump. Whinchats also lack the white neck patch of the male Stonechat. Typically perches on the tops of low vegetation such as bushes or weeds. In the Middle East breeds only in eastern Turkey, but occurs fairly widely on migration throughout the region, including Egypt.

102

Stonechat *Saxicola torquata* 12.5cm

The handsome male Stonechat, with rounded head, short tail and perky movements, especially its constantly flicking tail, is most likely to be seen perched prominently on a bush top. It is easily told by its blackish head with conspicuous white half neck-band and its orange underparts. The female has drab brownish and streaked head and upperparts, and a faint orange wash on the breast. Stonechats have a patchy distribution in the Middle East, breeding in Turkey and southern Arabia; in winter and on migration, found throughout most of the region, including Egypt.

Isabelline Wheatear *Oenanthe isabellina* 16cm

An upright, pale wheatear and one of the largest of the region, similar in size to Red-breasted Wheatear (*Oenanthe bottae*) of south-west Arabia. Most easily confused with the female or immature of Northern Wheatear, but note larger size, more upright stance, longer legs, and paler, more uniform grey-buff plumage; the tail also has a broader dark terminal band. A bird of open plains, semi-deserts and stony steppes. Breeds in Turkey and scattered regions of the east Mediterranean; otherwise occurs extensively on migration throughout the region, including Egypt.

103

Northern Wheatear *Oenanthe oenanthe* 15cm

Male (top); female (bottom)

The grey upperparts, black eye-mask and orange-buff breast of the male in spring distinguish it from all other wheatears that occur in the Middle East. The female and immatures are more difficult to identify, though the upperparts tend to show a greyish hue and the white tail has a fairly broad terminal band; these features, however, are subtle, and experience is needed to distinguish with confidence females and young of all wheatear species. In the region, Northern Wheatear breeds only in Turkey and the highlands of Israel, Lebanon and Syria, but it occurs widely on migration, including in Egypt.

Black-eared Wheatear *Oenanthe hispanica* 15cm

All female wheatears are difficult to identify, and best left to experienced observers. The beginner is advised to concentrate first on the males. The male Black-eared has two types, one with a black throat and the other with just a black patch through the eye; both have pale sandy back and black wings. Note the white rump and white tail sides, typical of most wheatears. Inhabits open rocky or lightly wooded country with scattered vegetation, but on passage also cultivated fields and semi-deserts. A summer visitor to the east Mediterranean and Turkey, and on migration found throughout much of the Middle East, including Egypt.

Desert Wheatear *Oenanthe deserti* 14cm

Despite its name, the Desert Wheatear is largely a winter visitor to most parts of the Middle East. It can be told from the region's other wheatears by its all-black tail and buffish-white rump. Plumage otherwise sandy-buff with black wings, which on the male join up with a black throat. Occurs in sandy or gravel steppes and semi-deserts, both when breeding and on migration. Mainly resident in its Middle East breeding areas of northern Egypt, Israel and nearby east Mediterranean countries, but also a passage migrant and winter visitor to much of the region.

Red-rumped Wheatear *Oenanthe moesta* 17cm

Yossi Eshbol

A rather large, active wheatear, the male and female of which differ markedly. The male has a black head with a white crown and nape, and greyish-black upperparts with white fringes to the wing-coverts; note especially the dark brown tail with rufous at base. The female is grey-brown above and buffish-white below, with a rufous-buff rump and sides of tail. A breeding resident of bushy desert fringes of northern Egypt and scattered areas in Jordan, Iraq, Syria, southern Israel and Arabia.

105

Mourning Wheatear *Oenanthe lugens* 14cm

A fairly small and stout, black and white wheatear. Rather similar to the Pied Wheatear (*Oenanthe pleschanka*), which in Egypt and the Middle East occurs only on migration. The Mourning Wheatear differs in having white on head confined to the crown (extends onto nape on Pied), black below confined to throat (extends onto upper breast on Pied), and orange-buff under-tail-coverts. A resident, often seen in pairs, in desolate, rocky country, including deserts and semi-deserts in Egypt, the east Mediterranean countries and north-west Arabia; it is absent in Turkey.

Hooded Wheatear *Oenanthe monacha* 17cm

The largest wheatear to occur in Egypt, with noticeably long tail, wings and bill. The male is a very smart black and white bird, the black on the head extending well down the breast and with just black corners to the white tail (no black tail-band). The female is sandy-brown and has a buffish (not white) rump and sides of tail, which, as on the male, lacks a black terminal band. Has a unique buoyant, butterfly-like flight when catching aerial insects. Inhabits rocky ravines and deserts. A resident of Egypt's Eastern Desert and Sinai, and scattered areas in Arabia, southern Israel and Jordan.

106

White-crowned Black Wheatear *Oenanthe leucopyga* 17cm

A large wheatear which is all black apart from a white crown, white rump and tail (except for black central feathers) and white under-tail-coverts. Young birds, as well as some females, have the crown entirely black. The other large wheatear in Egypt is the much rarer Hooded, the male of which has white underparts up to the breast and more extensive white on the head. A resident of many areas of Egypt, southern Israel, Jordan and parts of Arabia, where it occurs in rocky deserts and even around settlements and oases.

Rock Thrush *Monticola saxatilis* 19cm

The size of a small thrush with long bill and short tail, characters shown by all the rock thrushes. The male is quite striking, having blue-grey and rusty-red plumage with an 'unexpected' white panel on the back. The female is similar to female Blue Rock Thrush, but paler, with pale-spotted upperparts (plain on Blue Rock) and rusty-red tail (dark brown on Blue Rock). Unlike that species, Rock Thrush is only a summer visitor to the Middle East, where it breeds in the mountains of northern Israel, Syria and Turkey; it is fairly widespread on migration, including through Egypt.

107

Blue Rock Thrush *Monticola solitarius* 20cm

Approaching the Blackbird in size, the male is, as its name implies, dark blue. It may be shy and difficult to approach, and is most frequently seen perched on a rock in a prominent position. The female is dull brown, barred and spotted below. Mountain ranges, cliff faces and rocky deserts are this species' breeding areas, but it has a wide range of habitats on migration and in winter. A resident in scattered areas of the east Mediterranean; otherwise a migrant and winter visitor to most parts of the Middle East, including Egypt.

Blackbird *Turdus merula* 24cm

The male, all black with a yellow bill and yellow eye-ring, is a familiar bird to those living in Europe, but less so to inhabitants of the Middle East. The female and young males are all dark brown with a yellowish or dark bill. Seen both in trees and on the ground, where it runs in short bursts, stopping to look for food (worms are a particular favourite). Inhabits woodlands, gardens and plantations. In the Middle East, Blackbirds breed in Egypt's Nile Delta, Turkey and countries of the east Mediterranean; there is also an influx of migrants from the north in winter.

Song Thrush *Turdus merula* 23cm

The ground-feeding Song Thrush is a winter visitor to Egypt, along with two other thrushes. These are the scarcer Redwing (*Turdus iliacus*), which has white supercilium and rusty-red flanks, and the larger Fieldfare (*Turdus pilaris*), which has grey head and rump and reddish-brown back. The Song Thrush is easily told by its plain brown upperparts and its buffish-white underparts with neat black spots. In the Middle East, breeds only in woodlands in northern Turkey; elsewhere it is a winter visitor, but scarce in much of Arabia.

Fan-tailed Cisticola *Cisticola juncidis* 10cm

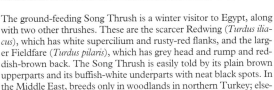

Alan Williams

A small warbler that is mostly seen and identified in flight, which is undulating and wide-ranging over grass, cereal or reed tops. Then, its characteristic song, a rhythmically repeated, almost metallic *pzit*, alerts the observer to its presence. When perched, it is a buffish warbler with bold dark streaking on its back; note also the white tips to the short tail when seen from below. Typically found in grain fields, grassy meadows and along the edges of marshes. Largely resident, with a patchy distribution in the Middle East, but in Egypt it is common in the Suez Canal region, Nile Delta and Nile Valley.

Graceful Prinia *Prinia gracilis* 10cm

A rather indistinct, small, grey-buff warbler with a long tail that is waved up and down and from side to side. Close views reveal a reddish-brown eye and lightly streaked upperparts. Difficult to see well as it is always very active, but the song, a monotonous, rhythmic *ze-vit...ze-vit...ze-vit...*, is distinctive and often the first indication of its presence. Inhabits scrub and low vegetation, often in villages and towns. A common resident in Egypt's Nile Delta and Valley and many coastal areas of the Middle East.

Scrub Warbler *Scotocerca inquieta* 10cm

A small, perky, ground-dwelling bird superficially similar to the Graceful Prinia, but its actions are quite distinct. Note the chunky body, large head with dark stripe through the eye and pale line above eye, and also the long tail cocked high as it hops on the ground, rather secretively and never far from cover. Occurs on stony hillsides and in semi-deserts with low scrub, often in mountains. A resident of Sinai and adjacent areas of Egypt's Eastern Desert, as well as parts of Israel, Syria, Jordan and Arabia.

Moustached Warbler *Acrocephalus melanopogon* 13cm

Very similar to the much commoner Sedge Warbler, another species that is found in reedbeds. A warm buff-brown bird with streaked upperparts, noticeable white stripe above the eye and dark crown. Sedge Warbler has a buffish-white stripe above the eye and is paler above. Note the rarer Moustached Warbler's habit of holding its tail raised (which Sedge Warbler rarely does). Occurs in reedbeds and swamps, nesting in reeds or bushes above shallow water. Breeds patchily in the Middle East, mainly in the east Mediterranean countries and Turkey; more widespread on passage and in winter, but uncommon in Egypt.

Richard Brooks

Sedge Warbler *Acrocephalus schoenobaenus* 13cm

Most likely to be confused with the Moustached Warbler, both having streaked upperparts and a conspicuous whitish stripe above the eye. Sedge, however, is paler above (Moustached being more reddish-brown), with a paler, streaked crown (blackish on Moustached). The call is a hard *tchek* and also a fast churring *trrr*. Found in reedbeds and overgrown wet areas, but on migration also in bushes away from water. In Egypt a passage migrant, as throughout most of the Middle East, apart from Turkey where it breeds.

European Reed Warbler *Acrocephalus scirpaceus* 13cm

A plain brownish warbler found almost entirely in reedbeds. Close views reveal a rusty tone to the rump, buff underparts, a pale line above the eye, a rather flat crown and a rounded tail. It is thus very like Marsh Warbler (*Acrocephalus palustris*), and separation of the two is not advised unless by their songs: European Reed Warbler has a monotonous, grating song on much the same pitch, whereas that of Marsh Warbler is musical, liquid and varied. A summer visitor to Egypt, where nesting is probably regular in the Nile Delta; also a widespread migrant in the Middle East, with a patchy breeding distibution.

Clamorous Reed Warbler *Acrocephalus stentoreus* 18cm

One of the two largest warblers to occur in the Middle East, the other being the very similar Great Reed Warbler (*Acrocephalus arundinaceus*). Both are essentially large brownish warblers inhabiting reedbeds, and are almost the size of a thrush; distinguishing between the two should not be attempted by inexperienced observers. They have similar loud, raucous songs. Clamorous is a common breeding resident in Egypt's Nile Delta and Valley, in parts of Arabia, where it also nests in mangroves on the Red Sea coast, and Israel.

Olivaceous Warbler *Hippolais pallida* 12cm

A medium-sized warbler and one of the commonest warblers in Egypt, but one that is also difficult to identify. You need to 'get your eye in' to attempt warbler identification. Olivaceous is olive-brown above with a slight greyish wash, and has a rather indistinct pale line above the eye; the underparts are buffish-white, with a white throat. The fairly large bill is brown, with a flesh-coloured lower mandible; the legs are greyish. On the breeding grounds, listen for its rhythmic, energetic song. Breeds commonly in Egypt and northern areas of the Middle East, and widespread on migration.

Olive-tree Warbler *Hippolais olivetorum* 15cm

Hadoram Shirihai

A large, greyish-brown warbler with square-ended tail, obvious pale wing panel and a heavy, yellowish bill. These features distinguish it from all other warblers, but good views are required because many members of the warbler family are difficult to identify. In the Middle East, it is a breeding summer visitor to the olive groves and oak woodlands of Turkey, Syria and northern Israel, passing through Egypt and neighbouring parts of the region on passage, but it is never commonly seen.

Spectacled Warbler *Sylvia conspicillata* 13cm

A small warbler, not unlike the Whitethroat, but smaller, shorter-tailed and brighter-coloured. The most noticeable feature is the rusty-red wing, shown by both males and females. Compared with Whitethroat, has a darker grey head, almost blackish in front of and around the eye. A bird of low scrub, in which it moves restlessly; also frequently seen hopping on the ground. The rattling *trrrrrr* call is often the first indication of its presence. In the Middle East confined largely to Israel, Jordan and Cyprus, where it is mostly resident; in Egypt an uncommon winter visitor, mostly to the north.

Subalpine Warbler *Sylvia cantillans* 12cm

A small warbler of scrubby hillsides, the male being easily identified by its ash-grey upperparts, deep reddish-orange underparts and noticeable white moustache. Close views reveal a red eye-ring. The song, given from bush top or in song flight, is fast and scratchy with clear and musical phrases. In the Middle East, breeds in low scrub, thickets and open woodland in western Turkey, where it is a summer visitor; in Egypt it is a passage migrant, as it is in most countries of the region, though usually scarce.

Ménétries's Warbler *Sylvia mystacea* 12cm

An active warbler of scrub and small trees which closely resembles the Sardinian Warbler. Separating females of the two species is extremely difficult, but male Ménétries's is told from male Sardinian by its black forehead and ear-coverts merging into its grey-brown upperparts (black head not clear-cut as on Sardinian); note also the pinkish wash on breast and throat demarcating a white moustache. The slightly shorter tail is frequently waved. Occurs in scrub, bushes on river edges and gardens. In the Middle East, breeds in eastern Turkey, parts of Iraq and Syria, where it is a summer visitor; more widespread in the region on passage, but rare in Egypt.

Sardinian Warbler *Sylvia melanocephala* 13cm

The male Sardinian Warbler is easily told by its shiny black head contrasting with white throat, grey body and noticeable red ring around the eye. For further distinctions, see Ménétries's Warbler. An active bird, often holding tail cocked, its presence often indicated by its frequent rattling, churring call. The females of the 'scrub warblers' are all very similar and not easily distinguishable by novice birdwatchers. Occurs in dry, bushy country, as well as in pine and evergreen-oak forests. In the Middle East, breeds in Turkey and neighbouring east Mediterranean countries, where it is a partial migrant; more widespread in the region, including Egypt, on passage and in winter.

Cyprus Warbler *Sylvia melanothorax* 13cm

Male

Female

The male is easily told by its white underparts marked with black bars and streaks, demarcated from the greyish upperparts by a white moustache. The female is similar to the female Sardinian Warbler, but usually shows dark crescent-shaped markings on throat and breast, as well as a white moustachial stripe. Breeds only in Cyprus, where it is a resident and partial migrant inhabiting rocky slopes with shrubs; otherwise a winter visitor to Israel and neighbouring countries, where it usually occurs in acacia woodland, and in Egypt an accidental visitor but probably overlooked.

Rüppell's Warbler *Sylvia rueppelli* 14cm

With its black head and throat with prominent white moustaches, this is one of the easiest warblers to identify. The female is duller but still shows a white moustache, though the head and throat are often mottled. A summer visitor to the Middle East, arriving at the end of March in southern and western Turkey, where it breeds in low scrub and bushes and can be quite common; on migration, found in Egypt and east Mediterranean countries, especially in acacia woodland.

116

Arabian Warbler *Sylvia leucomelaena* 14.5cm

A large warbler which is one of the Middle East's specialities. Most easily confused with the Orphean Warbler (*Sylvia hortensis*), but note Arabian's shorter wings, longer black tail with just white fringes at the sides, and dark eyes. Differs also in its habit of flopping its tail downwards or in a circular movement. Has a pleasant, loud warbling song, often the first indication of its presence. A resident warbler in Egypt, occurring largely in dry acacia woodland in the south-east; elsewhere in the region, found in Israel, Jordan and along the edge of the Red Sea.

Barred Warbler *Sylvia nisoria* 15cm

A large warbler with rather slow, heavy movements. The male in breeding plumage is unmistakable, having white underparts barred with dark crescents; note also the pale yellow iris, which gives a staring expression. The female is similar, but with markings less distinct. Young birds are not barred, and are rather sandy-greyish; they can be told by their large size, rather lumbering movements, pale fringes to the wing feathers and dark fringes to the undertail-coverts. A bird of thorny thickets, scattered trees and woodland clearings in Turkey, where it is a summer visitor; occurs on migration throughout the Middle East, including Egypt.

Lesser Whitethroat *Sylvia curruca* 13.5cm

This species is made up of several similar subspecies, some of which are considered to be full species in their own right. The Lesser Whitethroat illustrated here breeds in Turkey and parts of the east Mediterranean and occurs on migration throughout much of the Middle East, including Egypt. Note the grey plumage with a dark mask through the eye, the absence of any rufous in the wing, and the dark legs. The much paler Desert Lesser Whitethroat (form *minula*), with a washed-out appearance, is a winter visitor to Arabia, while the darker and stouter Hume's Lesser Whitethroat (form *althaea*) is an uncommon winter visitor to the Arabian Gulf.

Whitethroat *Sylvia communis* 14cm

A common medium-sized warbler, most closely resembling Spectacled Warbler and Lesser Whitethroat. It differs from the Spectacled Warbler in its larger size, longer tail, more evenly grey head and less rufous wings; and from Lesser Whitethroat in its rufous wings, orange legs, whiter eye-ring and more uniformly grey head. The short song, often uttered in dancing song flight, is a scratchy warbling. Occurs in scrub and bushy habitats. A breeding summer visitor to Israel (and areas to the north) and a passage migrant throughout the Middle East, including Egypt.

Blackcap *Sylvia atricapilla* 14cm

One of the commonest warblers to be seen in much of the Middle East, occurring mostly on passage. On its breeding grounds it is a fine songster. The male is easily told by its jet-black cap, as are the female and young birds by their reddish-brown cap. The somewhat similar Garden Warbler (*Sylvia borin*), which is also found on migration in the region, though less commonly, lacks the black or brown cap. In the Middle East, a summer visitor to the woodlands mainly of northern Turkey; otherwise a passage migrant throughout the region, including Egypt.

Male (top); female (bottom)

Eastern Bonelli's Warbler *Phylloscopus orientalis* 11cm

Bonelli's Warbler has recently been split into Western and Eastern Bonelli's. Both are similar to the Chiffchaff and Willow Warbler, and close views are needed for identification. About the size of Chiffchaff, but the plumage is greyish above and whitish below, with a plain face; note the green edgings to the wing and tail feathers and the greenish rump. The song is a characteristic trill and the call a short *chip*. A summer visitor to its Middle East breeding grounds in western and southern Turkey and isolated areas in Syria; occurs on migration in the east Mediterranean, including Egypt.

Willow Warbler *Phylloscopus trochilus* 11cm

This small, active, olive-coloured warbler is most easily confused with the Chiffchaff, both being common migrants in Egypt. Some birds are almost impossible to separate, but note the Willow Warbler's pale legs (dark on Chiffchaff), slightly longer wings and the more yellowish appearance, especially of young birds in autumn. The call, which is frequently uttered, is a soft *hueet*, slightly more disyllabic than that of Chiffchaff. Willow Warblers do not breed in the Middle East, but are common on migration in Egypt and throughout the region; they can occur in any area with trees.

Chiffchaff *Phylloscopus collybita* 11cm

The very similar-looking Chiffchaff and Willow Warbler are the two commonest 'leaf warblers' in the region. The Chiffchaff is the smaller of the two and is a rather drab grey-green, with generally less yellow in the plumage. It has dark legs, whereas those of Willow Warbler are pale. Both have a similar *hoo-eet* call, but the Chiffchaff's is almost monosyllabic. Found breeding in the Middle East only in northern and western Turkey and Syria, where it is a summer visitor to woodlands, but occurs on migration or as a winter visitor throughout the region, including Egypt.

Spotted Flycatcher *Muscicapa striata* 14cm

Flycatchers have a characteristic habit in which they fly upwards from their perch and manoeuvre in erratic circles for flying insects, then return usually to the same perch. The Spotted Flycatcher is brownish above, with pale streaks on the forehead and pale fringes to the wing feathers; it is whitish below, with a streaked breast. Breeds in parks, woodland edges and plantations, nesting on ledges in buildings or on a branch against a tree trunk. In the Middle East, it is a summer visitor to Turkey and parts of the east Mediterranean, but also a common migrant in Egypt and throughout much of the region.

Red-breasted Flycatcher *Ficedula parva* 12cm

The male in summer plumage is easily told by its Robin-like red upperbreast. It is otherwise grey-brown with white underparts and a black tail with white sides at the base. The female and young birds lack the red breast. Most birds in autumn look like this. An active and perky treedwelling bird, with tail often held cocked, but can easily disappear into the cover of branches and leaves and not be obvious. In the Middle East, a summer visitor to isolated areas of northern Turkey, where it breeds in deciduous forests; otherwise a rather rare migrant in the east Mediterranean, including Egypt.

Richard Porter

Collared Flycatcher *Ficedula albicollis* 13cm

The male is black above and white below, with a large white patch in the wing and a white collar around the neck. The female, young birds and winter males are brown above and white below, with a small white wing patch. Also occurring in the Middle East are the Pied Flycatcher and Semi-collared Flycatcher (*Ficedula hypoleuca* and *F. semitorquata*), and on migration (when they are not in breeding plumage) it is difficult to distinguish between the three. All are passage migrants through the east Mediterranean, including Egypt, and they can be found in any area with trees.

Fulvous Babbler *Turdoides fulvus* 25cm

Of the four species of babbler to occur in the Middle East, only the Fulvous Babbler and Arabian Babbler (*Turdoides squamiceps*) are found in Egypt. Both are thrush-like birds that live in small, often noisy groups; they have a long, graduated tail that is raised when hopping on the ground. The Fulvous is the warmer-coloured, with plain sandy-brown upperparts and paler underparts with a faint orange wash, while the Arabian is grey-brown and finely streaked. Fulvous Babbler is found in the Gebel Elba region in the southeast, and Arabian Babbler in Sinai.

Great Tit *Parus major* 14cm

Where it occurs in the Middle East, the Great Tit is one of the commonest and most obvious birds of woodland, where it nests in a hole in a tree. A large tit with a black cap, white cheeks, and yellow underparts with a broad black stripe down the middle. Young birds are duller, with yellowish cheeks. It has a wide range of calls based around a typical ringing and pleasant *chee-tweede-a-weet*. Will often gather in small flocks outside the breeding season. A resident of Turkey and east Mediterranean countries, including Egypt's Sinai.

Penduline Tit *Remiz pendulinus* 11cm

A small bird inhabiting trees at wetland fringes. Rather pale, with a characteristic black mask through the eye and a chestnut back. The bird's presence is often indicated by its thin, high *tsee* call, or by the sight of its nest; it builds an oval-shaped nest with an entrance tube at the side, suspended over water from the branches of a tree, especially a willow. Breeds in reedbeds and trees near wetlands in Turkey and Syria; in autumn birds disperse south, a few reaching Egypt.

123

Nile Valley Sunbird *Anthreptes metallicus*
10cm (summer male 15cm)

A small and very active sunbird with short, slightly decurved bill. Male in breeding plumage instantly identified by its greatly elongated central tail feathers, as well as glossy green upperparts with purple rump, blackish wings and tail, dark throat and breast, and yellow lower breast and belly. In winter, loses long tail feathers and bright colours and then like female and young birds, greyish-brown above and yellowish-white below, with white throat. Song of high-pitched thin trills and hisses. Found in gardens, dry scrub and acacia savanna. Resident in Nile Valley and in south-west and south Arabia.

Palestine Sunbird *Nectarinia osea* 11cm

Male   *Female*

A small, very active bird with a fairly long, decurved bill. The male in breeding plumage is blue-black with a metallic sheen, which can appear green in some lights. If you are very lucky, you will see orange tufts at the sides of the breast. Females and young birds are grey-brown with paler underparts. Like all sunbirds, it feeds on the nectar of flowers. The commonest and most familiar sunbird in the Middle East, the only region of the world in which it occurs, inhabiting well-vegetated areas from Lebanon south to Sinai and along the Red Sea coast, through Yemen to Oman, but in Egypt found only locally in Sinai.

124

Golden Oriole *Oriolus oriolus* 24cm

A thrush-sized bird found where there are large trees. The male, with its golden-yellow plumage and black wings, is unmistakable, but it can often be hard to see among the canopy foliage until it flies. The female is less distinct, being yellowish-green in coloration. In flight, which is fast, note the long, gentle undulations, somewhat reminiscent of a woodpecker. The song is a mellow, fluty *too-lee-too-lee*, easily remembered once heard. A summer visitor to the Middle East, breeding in Turkey, Cyprus and northern Syria, but occasionally in isolated areas farther south; it can be seen on passage throughout, including in Egypt.

Red-backed Shrike *Lanius collurio* 17cm

The shrikes are also known as 'butcher birds', because they often impale the insects and small animals (including birds) that they catch on thorns in a favourite tree. This is known as their 'larder'. The male Red-backed Shrike has a blue-grey head contrasting with reddish-brown back and a black mask through the eye. The female is duller, with just a faint mask through the eye and dark scallop-shaped marks on the whitish underparts. A summer visitor to its Middle East breeding grounds in Turkey and parts of the east Mediterranean; otherwise a passage migrant in spring and autumn throughout the region, including Egypt.

125

Lesser Grey Shrike *Lanius minor* 20cm

Care is needed to separate this species from the very similar Southern Grey Shrike, especially in spring and autumn, when they both occur on migration. The Lesser Grey is best told by the broad black band across its forehead (forehead grey on Southern Grey Shrike) and the pink wash on its underparts; it also has proportionately longer wings and shorter tail than Great Grey. During migration periods, shrikes are one of the typical birds of roadside telegraph wires and close views can often be obtained. A migrant through Egypt and other parts of the Middle East, but breeds only in Turkey.

Southern Grey Shrike *Lanius meridionalis* 26cm

Richard Porter

Very similar to the Great Grey Shrike (*Lanius excubitor*) of northern Europe, and only recently 'split' from that species by taxonomists. Note its grey upperparts, white underparts and prominent black markings: black mask through the eye, and black wings and tail. It differs from the very similar Lesser Grey Shrike in its larger size, shorter wings and grey forehead. A breeding bird of much of Egypt, the east Mediterranean (except Turkey) and parts of Arabia; those breeding in Asia migrate to the region in winter.

Woodchat Shrike *Lanius senator* 18cm

A very distinctive shrike in adult plumage, having chestnut head, black back and tail and large white wing patches. In flight, note the white rump. Young birds are more difficult to identify, being rather similar to young Red-backed and Masked Shrikes, and are best told from Red-backed by their creamy shoulder patches and rump. A fine songster, with clear whistles and much mimicry of other birds. A summer visitor to east Mediterranean countries and south and west Turkey; occurs on migration throughout the Middle East, including Egypt.

Masked Shrike *Lanius nubicus* 18cm

The adult is a handsome bird with its black and white plumage and orange-yellow wash on the sides of the underparts. It has a longer-tailed appearance than the other shrikes. The young birds are not easy to distinguish from young Woodchat Shrikes, both having whitish shoulder patches, but they are greyer (less brown), with longer tail and finer bill. The breeding range of the Masked Shrike is almost entirely confined to the Middle East, where it is a summer visitor to east Mediterranean countries and south and west Turkey; on spring and autumn migration found throughout the region, including Egypt, where more common in spring.

House Crow *Corvus splendens* 43cm

Look for this dark grey and black crow on Egypt's Red Sea coast and coastal areas of Arabia, especially around ports. It superficially resembles the Hooded Crow, but the grey is darker and the back is black; it is also slightly smaller and slimmer, with a long, deep bill and domed crown. Does not occur naturally in the Middle East, where the colonies are the result of introductions from India in the last 30 years, the birds probably having arrived on grain boats. In Egypt, breeds mainly in towns along the Suez Canal and Gulf of Suez.

Brown-necked Raven *Corvus ruficollis* 50cm

A large black bird, very similar to the Raven (*Corvus corax*), but the two are largely geographically isolated. Egypt is one of the few countries where both occur: the much rarer Raven on the north coast and the desert-loving Brown-necked Raven commonly throughout much of the country. Brown-necked Raven can be told from Raven by its slimmer wings, longer bill and bronzy-brown sheen on the hindneck, but this sheen can be difficult to see. When perched, note the Brown-necked's longer wings, reaching the tail-tip. A widespread breeding bird of Arabia, Jordan and Israel.

Fan-tailed Raven *Corvus rhipidurus* 47cm

Richard Porter

Slightly smaller and chunkier than the Brown-necked Raven, and with a stout bill. It is most easily recognized by its short tail, and in flight, when soaring, it can look almost tailless as the fanned tail merges into the hindwing. Like the Brown-necked, a bird of semi-deserts, cliffs and crags, often near human habitation and especially rubbish dumps. Resident in Sinai and south-east Egypt, and elsewhere in the Middle East in Israel, Jordan and western and southern Arabia, from sea level to 3000m.

Hooded Crow *Corvus corone cornix* 47cm

A grey and black crow, the body being grey with a black head and throat, and the wings and tail black. Breeds solitarily, but outside the breeding season often forms large roosts at night along with Jackdaws (*Corvus monedula*), a smaller black crow with a grey hindneck and pale eye that occurs in the region mainly in Turkey. Hooded Crow is found in open country with scattered trees, where it builds a large nest of sticks high in a tree or on a pylon. A resident in Egypt, notably along the Nile Valley and Delta, and in Turkey and east Mediterranean countries.

129

Tristram's Grackle *Onychognathus tristramii* 25cm

Grackles are members of the starling family. Larger than the better-known Starling, and with a glossy black plumage and orange wing patches in flight. The female is duller, with a greyish-brown head. A noisy bird, often gathering in flocks to feed on fruits. The far-carrying call resembles a wolf-whistle. Nests mainly in crevices on rock faces. The world range of this grackle is confined to the Middle East, where it is a resident of Egypt's Sinai, Israel, Jordan and western and southern Arabia; occurs from sea level to 3,000 m.

Starling *Sturnus vulgaris* 22cm

Blackish with purple and green gloss and yellow bill in breeding season. In winter, has pale spots (tips of the feathers) over entire plumage. The young birds (until early autumn) are dull brownish-grey with a black bill. A familiar bird throughout its breeding range, and in autumn and winter often in large flocks which roost communally, sometimes in tens of thousands. It occurs in a range of habitats, but especially in or near towns and villages, where it nests in a hole or crevice. In the Middle East breeds in Turkey; in winter, numbers are swollen by migrants from the north and birds will then occur throughout much of the region, including Egypt.

House Sparrow *Passer domesticus* 15cm

A familiar bird in many towns and villages in the Middle East, nesting in hole in building or in similar crevice. The male and female differ: note male's black bib, white cheeks, grey crown and reddish-brown hindneck, and female's rather plain greyish-brown coloration with pale stripe above the eye and dark stripes on back and wings. The Tree Sparrow (*Passer montanus*), very rare in Egypt, differs from House Sparrow in its red-brown cap and black spot on white cheeks. Widespread resident breeder, occurring in areas of habitation and cultivation throughout many areas of Egypt and most of the region.

Spanish Sparrow *Passer hispaniolensis* 15cm

Similar to the House Sparrow, but the male is quite distinct with its chestnut crown and heavy black streaking on back and underparts. This pattern is far less marked in the winter. Female is almost impossible to tell from the female House Sparrow. Breeds colonially, often in large numbers, building a domed nest with entrance hole at side in a tall tree, or even in the base of a White Stork's nest. Breeds in Turkey, east Mediterranean countries and limitedly in Arabia; occurs more widely in winter, when a common visitor to Egypt, often in large flocks.

Male (top); female (bottom)

131

Avadavat *Amandava amandava* 9cm

Male   *Female*

This small, short-tailed finch is a native of India that has colonized the area following the escape of birds from captivity, as it is a popular cagebird. The male in breeding plumage is bright crimson, with a blackish tail, and with small white spots on underparts and wing-coverts. The female is brown, with a red rump and bill. Its habitat requirements are varied, but it is present in trees and bushes, usually near water and often close to human habitation. Breeds in the Nile Delta and neighbouring areas and sporadically in Arabia.

Chaffinch *Fringilla coelebs* 15cm

The male chaffinch is an attractive bird with its buff-orange under-parts, grey crown and nape, and white shoulder patch, wingbar and outer tail feathers. The female is much duller, rather brownish, but also shows the white wing and tail markings of the male. Feeds mostly on the ground, and in winter often gathers in large flocks with other finches and buntings to forage in cultivated fields. In the Middle East, breeds in woodland in Turkey, Cyprus and north-west Syria, but in winter migrates south to east Mediterranean countries, some reaching Egypt.

European Serin *Serinus serinus* 12cm

Another small finch with a stubby bill, occurring in pairs or small flocks. The male is told by its canary-yellow face and breast, bold streaks on its flanks and, in flight, its yellow rump. Females are much duller, showing barely any yellow except on the rump. One of the best identification features is the call, a fast, trilling *tirrililit*. The song, often given in bat-like flight, is fast, musical and jingling. A bird of parks, orchards and woodland edges and, in winter, adjacent fields and wasteland. In the Middle East, it is mainly resident in Turkey and east Mediterranean countries; larger numbers occur in the winter, when birds reach Egypt.

Greenfinch *Carduelis chloris* 15cm

Male   *Female*

A large, dull yellowish-green finch (female browner) with distinctive yellow patches on wings and tail and a stout flesh-pink bill. The song, often uttered in bat-like display flight, is a musical twittering. Semi-colonial in the breeding season, but often in flocks with other seed-eaters in winter. Occurs in farmland, plantations, parks and oases, nesting in a low tree. In the Middle East, it is a resident of Turkey and east Mediterranean countries, including Egypt, where it breeds in the north; commoner in winter, when migrants arrive from the north.

European Goldfinch *Carduelis carduelis* 14cm

One of the most distinctive birds in Egypt and the northern part of the Middle East (absent from the south). Easily identified by its red face, black and white head pattern, and black wings with conspicuous broad yellow wingbar, the latter especially noticeable in flight. Note also the 'dancing' flight and tinkling liquid flight call. A bird of orchards, gardens, farmland with trees and waste ground, where often seen in small groups feeding on thistles. In Egypt, mainly resident in the Nile Delta and Valley.

Linnet *Carduelis cannabina* 14cm

A sprightly finch, the male of which is easily identified in the breeding season by its red forehead, two red breast patches, chestnut back, and white wing-flashes when it flies. At other times of the year, the male resembles the female and young birds, being dull greyish-brown with a streaked breast; but in all plumages shows the white wing-flashes in flight. Often seen in small flocks, occurring in open country with trees and scrub. Breeds in Turkey and parts of the east Mediterranean, areas to which it is also a winter visitor, as it is to Egypt.

Trumpeter Finch *Bucanetes githagineus* 13cm

Male

Female

A rather inconspicuous, ground-dwelling finch with a large head, short tail and stout bill. The male in breeding plumage has an orange-red bill, and is grey-buff with a pinkish wash on underparts, wings and forehead. Females and juvenile birds are simply sandy grey-buff with a yellowish-brown bill. Note that, in all plumages, the legs are orange-coloured. Trumpeter Finches take their name from their wheezing, nasal song. Occurs on rather barren, rocky hillsides and plains. In Egypt this is a breeding resident of many areas, as it is, patchily, throughout the Middle East.

Common Rosefinch *Carpodacus erythrinus* 14cm

The female and juvenile are drab brownish finches, stout-billed and with well-streaked underparts and two pale wingbars. The adult male is more likely to be recognized, having a red crown, face and breast. Nests semi-colonially, and the first indication of its presence is often the song: a clear whistle in three parts, *wheety-wheety-wee*. Occurs in wooded mountains, usually near streams and wet valley bottoms. A summer visitor to its breeding grounds in northern Turkey; on migration, rather scarce in Egypt and neighbouring east Mediterranean countries.

135

Sinai Rosefinch *Carpodacus synoicus* 14cm

Male (top); female (bottom)

One of the Middle East's specialities, and the national bird of Jordan, although it is named after Egypt's Sinai. The male is easily told by its crimson-pink plumage with frosty streaking on crown and ear-coverts; the upperparts are grey-brown with a mauve tinge. Females and juveniles are a drab grey-buff with faint streaking and with a ginger wash on the face; they show no wingbars. Rather nervous in behaviour and often in groups, especially in winter. Its breeding range is confined to a small area of Sinai, southern Israel and southern Jordan, where it occurs in barren, rocky hills.

Hawfinch *Coccothraustes coccothraustes* 18cm

Tim Loseby

A large, robust finch with a deep, powerful bill. Note its short tail with white tip, white shoulder patches and, in flight, a white stripe through the flight feathers. The bill is lead-grey in summer and pale in winter. A rather secretive bird of deciduous forests and orchards, but often in small groups, especially on migration. In the Middle East, breeds only in a few areas of western Turkey; in autumn, birds from Europe migrate into the region for the winter, and some reach northern Egypt.

136

House Bunting *Emberiza striolata* 14cm

Superficially resembles a small Rock Bunting (*Emberiza cia*), which does not occur in Egypt, but differs in its orange lower mandible, bright rufous upperparts, more finely streaked dull grey crown and throat, and rufous (not white) outer tail feathers. The female is duller, with an even more diffuse head pattern. A resident of rather desolate rocky and sandy wadis with little vegetation, nesting in a hole or crevice in a rock face or building. It breeds very locally in Egypt's Sinai and Eastern Desert and patchily elsewhere in the Middle East; where it does occur, it can be quite common.

Cinereous Bunting *Emberiza cineracea* 17cm

A nondescript and rather rare bunting whose distribution is confined to the Middle East. The male has a greenish-yellow wash to the head, but is otherwise greyish; the female is darker and even duller, heavily streaked and with a yellowish-green tinge on the throat. Differs further from Ortolan Bunting and Cretzschmar's Bunting in its greyish (not pinkish) bill. A summer visitor to dry, rocky areas, mainly in southern Turkey, up to the tree limit; its migration through the region is little known, but it is very rare in Egypt.

Ortolan Bunting *Emberiza hortulana* 17cm

The male has a green-grey head and upper breast, a yellow moustache and throat, streaked upperparts and chestnut underparts. Note particularly the pale eye-ring. The female, much drabber and with finely streaked crown and upper breast, is best separated from other buntings by its yellowish moustache and eye-ring. A largely ground-dwelling bunting, occurring in small flocks on migration. A summer visitor to its Middle East breeding grounds in Turkey; widespread on passage throughout the region, including Egypt, where it is common, especially in spring.

Cretzschmar's Bunting *Emberiza caesia* 15cm

Male

Female

Resembes Ortolan Bunting, but with a blue-grey head and with the yellow on the face replaced by orange. The female is like a drab version of the male, and young birds are very like Ortolans but with a more rusty hue. Is frequently first located by its simple but often repeated song of three or four notes, *dsi-dsi-dsi dsiu*, the last note slightly lower. A bird of rocky hillsides, usually with scattered bushes, but on migration will inhabit farmland and desert fringes. A summer visitor to southern Turkey and the east Mediterranean, with migration through Egypt.

Reed Bunting *Emberiza schoeniclus* 16cm

Alan Williams

The male is easily told by its black head and bib, white moustache and collar, and reedbed habitat. The female is streaked brownish, with a pale stripe above the eye, and a broad whitish moustache bordered on each side by a black streak. In the Middle East, this bunting is a scattered breeding resident at wetlands with reedbeds in Turkey; in winter, more northerly populations migrate south into the region and it can then be quite common in reedy areas in the east Mediterranean, but rarely reaches Egypt.

Corn Bunting *Miliaria calandra* 18cm

A stout, rather drab bunting with a thick pale yellowish bill and streaked plumage, showing a broad buffish band above the eye. Male and female are similar, but the male characteristically dangles its legs when flying between songposts. The monotonous song is rather like the jangling of a set of keys. Occurs in cultivation, mountain steppes and meadows. Largely resident on its Middle East breeding grounds in Turkey and the east Mediterranean; more widespread in winter, when migrants arrive from Europe and Asia, and then fairly common in Egypt.

Glossary

coverts The small feathers at base of quill feathers forming main flight surfaces of wing and tail

endemic Indigenous species restricted to a particular area

eyebrow Contrasting line above eye (supercilium)

eye-stripe Contrasting line through eye

flank Side of the body

gregarious Frequently occurring in groups

migrant Non-resident traveller

necklace A line of markings around front of neck

orbital ring Unfeathered bare ring around eye

primaries The main outer flight feathers (show as longest part of folded wing)

race Another name for subspecies

resident Remaining in a local area throughout year

roost Resting or sleeping place

secondaries The inner flight feathers on rear half of wing

subspecies A population which is morphologically different from other populations of same species

supercilium A stripe above eye (eyebrow)

terminal At the end or tip

underparts Undersurface of body from throat to undertail-coverts

undertail-coverts Small feathers below tail covering bases of tail feathers

underwing-coverts Small underwing feathers covering bases of primaries and secondaries

upperparts Upper surface of body

vent Area around anus, including undertail-coverts

wingbar A visible line of colour at tips of wing-coverts

wing-coverts Small feathers on wing covering bases of primaries and secondaries

Further reading

If this book has whetted your appetite, then you may want to learn more about the birds of the general Middle East or the UAE in particular. The following titles are recommended reading and reference books:

Aspinall, S.J. *Status & Conservation of the Breeding Birds of the United Arab Emirates*. (3rd edition due 2006).

Evans, M.I. *Important Bird Areas in the Middle East*. BirdLife International, 1994.

Hellyer, P. & S.J. Aspinall. *The Emirates – A Natural History*. Trident Press, UK, 2005.

Porter, R.F., S. Christensen & P. Schiermacker-Hansen. *Field Guide to the Birds of the Middle East* T & AD Poyser, London, 1996.

Useful addresses

Ornithological Society of the Middle East & Caucasus (OSME) c/o The Lodge, Sandy, Bedfordshire, SG19 2DL, UK. http://www.osme.org

Emirates Bird Records Committee, c/o P.O. Box 45553, Abu Dhabi, UAE. Email: ebrcuae@gmail.com Please send a record of your observations to EBRC at the above email address.

EBRC recorder's website: www.tommypedersen.com (This website has photographs of a large selection of birds, maps and directions for a host of birdwatching sites, and other useful information for visitors)

Twitchers' Guide (a weekly round-up of bird sightings in UAE) available online via: www.uaeinteract.com

Bird tours around the UAE can easily be arranged. Please check the email addresses and websites above, or telephone UAE +971(0)50-6424357/8. The weekend in UAE is now Friday and Saturday, which is consequently the best time to schedule a visit should you wish to be escorted by a resident guide.

Index

143

144